PSYCHIC HEALER

Noel Street, Psychic Healer

PSYCHIC HEALER

by
Judy Dupree

Published by CSA Press
Lakemont, Ga. 30552

Standard Book Number 0-87707-094-6

Printed in the United States of America
by CSA Press, Lakemont, Ga. 30552

This book is dedicated to those friends who have brought the Spirit of Healing into my life, and to all Healers everywhere who seek to balm the suffering of Mankind.

"In deep appreciation to Jean Leighton of Miami, Florida for healing illustrations within this book."

TABLE OF CONTENTS

FOREWORD

Noel Street has proved to be one of those rare individuals who not only speaks of spiritual gifts but is quite capable in demonstrating them for the benefit of his Brother Man. Time and time again have I witnessed his ability to ease suffering through psychic healing and reincarnation 'tracings' — channeled through his remarkable faculty of Dual Consciousness.

Humble in spirit, he stays in the background as much as these gifts will allow and seeks only to serve Spirit where he is most needed.

As my teacher and friend, he has led me with great patience and longsuffering. And it is with deep respect and devotion that I have sought, through this modest volume, to pay tribute to his unusual and valuable ministry to the world.

J.C.D.

SECTION I

THE HEALING MINISTRY
OF NOEL STREET

Chapter 1

The End and the Beginning

Wimpole Street seemed far-removed that night as people streamed down the isles and sat motionless on the wooden chairs before the hushed audience.

In an almost secretive glance, I squinted at the tall, straight healer who stood behind a rather plump woman on the platform and mysteriously moved his hands several inches from her body as though he were warming his fingers. A prayer was offered up to the "Healing Angels" asking for the easement of suffering, and I remember feeling an overwhelming attunement with the invisible host of Helpers to whom this miracle worker spoke with great reverence.

Normally, I would have been absent from a gathering which pre-labeled its activities within the realm of spiritual healing. However, certain facts had lodged in my head about this psychic healer named Noel Street, so that I put aside my prejudice for awhile and left my mind slightly ajar.

First of all, I knew that this man was a typically conservative Englishman who was neither an emotional type nor a syrupy religionist whose primary aim was to please and finally *squeeze* a living out of the gullible or the desperate.

Being the grandson of an eminent London physician, he had early accepted orthodox medicine as a matter of course. While still a young boy, Noel saw his father sent to a hospital for "Incurables," a crisis which forced drastic changes in his domestic environment. Yet the whole household seemed to make the necessary adjustments quite well.

It was not until many years later in another country that he turned from the dictates of modern medicine and began to seek a different source of help in spiritual healing, which ultimately opened up a whole new avenue of experience for him.

A Young Boy Questions the Church and Society

Being subject to a very orthodox upbringing in a Plymouth Brethren Church in Hampshire, England, Noel Street had been reluctant to accept certain dogmas which had been offered to him as a child. When quizzed on why he did not readily believe the lessons of his church school, he replied in his childlike but wise manner: "Because you say that it is wrong for the Indians to worship trees!"

Due to the society in which he grew up, he remembers being served a generous portion of English thought on aristocracy. Unbothered by this societal distraction, he simply ignored it and went his own way.

As a rather independent and resourceful child, Noel's greatest pleasure was to escape into the woods around Sussex. Arising at 4:00 a.m. the boy would pack a few matches and some food to take along on the early morning trek through the sleeping town. All the way to the edge of the forest, his mind practically burst with the thought, "Today I will find a place where no white man has ever been!" And in his childish reverie, he would wander off the beaten path, chopping his way into a thick vegetative shelter of green.

Here he would sit for hours, drinking deeply of nature's lovely colors and forms as the sun rose, revealing the wood's most delicate wild flowers and exquisite birds.

Such a love of nature seemed to usher this boy child into incarnation. And so he grew into manhood, steeped in the belief that all creation is of God and greatly to be revered.

A New Country

Many years later when he had immigrated to New Zealand and had children of his own, Noel sought that same sense of solitude in the native "bush" country.

As the manager of a rapidly growing food plant in Auckland, he was able to initiate many new ideas in his field. Caught in this web-like structure of commerce, most of this businessman's energies were spent in "getting ahead."

Then came the blow that stopped all operations in his own personal world. Angela, his two-year-old daughter, was stricken with some unnamed disease, which left her frail little body in an outbreak of ulcers. To make matters worse, the condition began to retard her mentally so that she verged on idiocy.

Various medical treatments and endless visits to the hospital produced nothing more than weariness and a growing sense of frustration and fear. As a last resort measure, the father took his child to a spiritual healer named Leslie Tasman Symons. Within a few weeks following healing treatment, the little girl had made a complete recovery.

An illness of one year's duration was gone almost instantly, and to express his appreciation to the man who had channeled Angela's healing, Mr. Street began to attend the weekly meetings of Leslie Symons. Never suspecting that he would actually participate in the healing services, his new friend immediately called him to the platform 'to help.'

Week after week, Symons seemed to derive great pleasure from Noel's support and assistance as a healer. The patients, likewise, began to expect to see this new healer alongside Symons. And thus, a partnership was formed in a gradual and unassuming way. Little did Noel suspect that his days in the commercial world were numbered.

A New Vocation

In Rev. Street's own words, ''Whenever a man with a family decides to leave the security of a good job and begin something completely new, his decision must be based in strong conviction.'' Indeed, his own faith in Spirit never slackened, and very shortly his mind was made up — he wanted to serve as a full-time healer.

This new role was one with which he could never have identified prior to his daughter's healing, yet he seemed to fill the place with a natural ease. From the beginning of his interest in spiritual development, his psychic powers unfolded in a unique manner. Early initiatory phases of his training from Spirit took the form of magnificient nightly visions, usually accompanied with specific instructions to be carried out. In seeing the discipline that has been required of this healer, I marvel not only at his amazing gifts but equally at the perseverance that preceded their development.

The Maori Days

Early in his career, Rev. Street had the rare privilege of serving the brown-skinned Maori people of New Zealand. It was during this most treasured era of his life that he stored an abundance of happy memories.

"The relationship between the Maoris and myself was always based on a deep mutual respect," says Rev. Street. "Any prejudice which I may have taken with me as part of my early conditioning was quickly shattered by my association with them. I was with them in their laughter and tears — saw many born and some die, and this sharing developed a great love between us."

On one occasion while he was healing among the natives, an old Maori man approached him who was suffering with great whelps and open sores on his leg. He had attempted to cure them in every way possible, but his efforts were in vain. The pride which he felt towards his own race was so great that the prospect of seeking a white healer was abominable to him. However, this particular distaste was finally overcome only by the excruciating pain which he was experiencing. So the old Maori tribesman swallowed his pride and made his way to the healing clinic.

Understanding the ambivalance that stirred within his Brother, the healer gently laid his hand on the afflicted leg. Immediately, a great surge of power shot through the old man's limb with an audible CRACK! so that he cried out in fright and surprise!

As the two men looked at each other in amazement, they quietly shared the realization of Universal Power, breaking down the barriers between man and man. Within a few days, the Maori joyously returned to the clinic to expose a leg which was completely clear of the earlier blemishes.

Transformation into Etheric Matter

It was here among these people that Noel learned much of their customs, beliefs, and practices — especially related to psychic phenomena. One such belief of the Maoris is that the spirits of discarnate relatives can take the form of birds, appearing to be of a physical substance but actually composed of etheric matter. This transformation quite often is effected to warn them of approaching danger.

A story is told by Rev. Street concerning a young Maori woman whom he met in a boarding house in New Zealand. As he sat before the fire on a cold winter day, the girl approached him and exclaimed rather openly, "Mr. Street, I have some of the same powers that you have!"

as a person learns of the spiritual laws under which
he lives. This understanding can help speed up his
spiritual progress on the pathway of life.

Furthermore, most people who seek knowledge of
their past lives for the sake of spiritual guidance
usually receive abundant light on their individual
pathways.

A Wife's Karma

A close friend of mine married a man who later
became an alcoholic. In trying to raise their small
children and deal with the inherent problems in this
relationship, she experienced a great deal of heartache
and woe. At one point she was tempted to leave her
husband because of the pressures which were upon
her. However, putting her Spiritual will to work,
she eventually overcame the difficulties of the physical
plane by living more within the spiritual realm.

Of course, this process took time, for thought patterns which have been set up over a period of years
are not changed in a week. But through living one
day at a time, this woman was able to change herself and her own thinking to the point of completely
changing the direction of her whole life.

Her husband, along with the children, responded
quite well to the new aura of love and peace which
was poured out from Spirit and channeled through
this woman. Fifteen years later, the family has become a signpost of great encouragement as they extend much love and understanding toward people
who are having similar emotional problems which
they themselves experienced in earlier years.

About a year ago, this woman was privileged to have a reincarnation reading of her past lives by Rev. Street, who had no knowledge of her present life whatsoever.

One of the first lives which he viewed for her explained the reason for her present karma. She had been born in France in the 18th century and had sought extremes for her happiness. Finally, in marriage she chose a man who later became addicted to alcohol; throughout the remainder of her life she had abhorred this habit and illness in him and had left him after several years of marriage. Never did she use the power of her spiritual nature to help understand or ease the karma under which they lived.

As a result of failing to overcome this problem which a physical life had set before her, she was required to return to a similar situation and experience it again as an opportunity to use her Spiritual will. As was in evidence by the events of her present life, this woman had not only worked out her karma but used the experience to serve her Brother Man! Such is the message of rebirth — not only physically, but spiritually as well.

This example is only one of many which is evidence of karmic patterns set up and brought into the present life.

Unusual Demonstrations on Radio and Television

One distinguishing mark of Rev. Street's ministry is that he is probably the only living man who has ever publicly demonstrated on radio and television his remarkable ability of looking backwards

in time. His television debut in America was on
the "fearsome" Joe Pyne Show. Since then, he has
appeared hundreds of times over public media and
thrilled audiences in many parts of the world.

As people have seen and heard of this unusual
gift, whole families have gone to him for reincarnation
readings, often taking infants for the purpose of vocational guidance.

One such family to seek the benefits of his ability
to trace past lives was the physicist and his wife
mentioned earlier who have seven children. Seeking
this knowledge of past lives in relation to the present
has been an immeasurable aid to each family member. As the oldest daughter said, "The readings for
our family were of great help in directing us toward
suitable vocations, as well as uncovering certain
problems which had not been explainable. Generally,
we were all able to understand our individual karma,
and it was a thrilling experience for the whole family!"

Each week brings many letters to Rev. Street
concerning the fact that reincarnation readings have
real value in increasing understanding and easing
difficult circumstances.

One such letter came from Australia:

"Dear Rev. Street,

Thank you for an excellent reading. This is really a
slum clearance project, my past being slums, and
you, the one enabling me to see how an area must
be levelled for new foundations to be laid; when this is
done, I shall eventually be of use to the right forces, so
you are doing much more than merely pointing out landmarks to a tourist . . . ."

Another gentlemen from South Africa writes expressing his gratitude in understanding himself better:

"Dear Sir,

The survey of my past lives, which you have drawn up for me, was delivered at my home on Christmas Eve. Let me say quite plainly that it was the most wonderful Christmas present I have ever received. . . .You are quite right regarding the negative qualities in my past, because some of them are still my weaknesses in this life, but now I have the courage to try and overcome them with God's help.

I wish to thank you a thousand times for what I consider a most accurate and fascinating revelation!"

These letters are only two examples of cases wherein reincarnation readings have given the added impetus of correcting those personal imperfections which block spiritual progress.

Particularly am I grateful for this strong arm of Noel Street's outreach, for it was with his guidance through the help of a reading that I received healing for both the mind and body.

Finding myself quite distraught over a lack of satisfying answers which various philosophies and religions had handed me, I began to tell a close friend of the turmoil which was constantly erupting within me. Perhaps I had reached a new plateau of readiness, for Spirit directed me at that moment into an unfamiliar area of thought and experience.

As the friend listened, he recognized my queries as being directly related to the belief in reincarnation, in which he himself was firmly grounded. As he explained the necessity of returning again and again to the earth plane in order to benefit from certain experiences for our learning, my heart began to pound ecstatically!

It seemed that all the fears of so many years dropped from me, and for the first time in this life was I free and able to soar, to feel real joy, and to replace an overwhelming fear of God with true reverence, love and adoration!

For me, this discovery was a prelude to the joyous strain of my soul: "Ye shall know the truth, and truth will make you free!"

And never has this new-found song lessened in its hold upon my heart. It has served to illumine my pathway more each day, offering a new depth of meaning in the awareness that we are all God's children, and that "all His sons will one day reach His feet, however far they stray!" A lost soul is an impossibility.

Music to My Ears

Within a week Spirit led me further in this new adventure. I dropped in unexpectedly to visit a friend named Mary Jane, and she was unusually excited that day.

"I've got something to tell you!" she spouted out. And quickly she brought out a tape recording.

Without giving me time for questions, she went on about ". . . a man who can look backward . . . Noel Street! . . . and a reincarnation reading. . . .

Slowly, I began to piece the words together and understood that a man named Noel Street in New

York had traced back some of her past lives. Having a growing belief in continuous incarnations myself, I was intrigued by the notion that anyone could possibly possess such a faculty of looking backwards in time. So I asked her if we could listen to the tape together.

Sitting down and hardly knowing what to expect, I strained my ears, determined to hear every word that the 'voice' repeated. As the tracing began, Rev. Street was seeing my friend in 'what was your most recent life. . . . You lived in Germany in the 19th century . . . a female who loved music and dancing. . ."

With those words out, a strange song from a music box began to play in the room where the two of us sat, and our attention was immediately jerked back in wonder and surprise!

"Where is that music coming from?" we both queried simultaneously! Switching off the recorder, Mary Jane spotted a little music box on the dresser which had somehow been released, even though the lid had not been lifted; and it was playing a song — a *German* melody, in fact!

Attempting to stop the sound, she found that the box was mysteriously jammed and had to run down before it would cut off.

Coincidence? Perhaps. But it was strange that the box had never before — or has since — jammed. Whatever the explanation one may apply, I must add that the remainder of Mary Jane's reading held great interest for me. And somehow I left that day with a deeper conviction in the validity of reincarnation.

Within a week, I had received a tracing of my own lives from Rev. Street and was amazed at the unmistakable resembling patterns which flowed from the account of the past into my present life.

It can never be emphasized enough that one will receive from a reading no more and no less than what he asks. When one desires this help from Rev. Street solely out of curiosity about the past, no doubt he will be dealt no more than a review of geographical locations, dates, cultures, and such details of by-gone experiences.

While on the last tour across the country, the Street caravan had halted temporarily in a large city. As is usually the case, we found that the sponsors for the public meetings had completely booked the appointment time prior to our arrival.

As one woman sat patiently waiting for an 'Akashic Life Reading,' I noticed on the application form that she had stated her reason for wanting the tracing to be 'curiosity.' I explained that Rev. Street did not trace past lives for that purpose — he required a more solid approach, such as understanding karma.

As quickly as I had challenged her motive, she retorted with equal speed: "Oh, well, that's what I'm curious about — my karma!" Needless to say, she got her reading and we got a good laugh!

Quite different from her light approach, I sought through my reading to know the purpose of my life — a question which desperately gnawed on me from the inside. And inevitably the understanding and direction came, accompanied by an inherent healing of the mind. And from that guidepost onward in my journeying, I have never been required to return to the old way of thinking that had cultured and grown

Noel on television.

Noel speaking on Rebirth to a capacity audience in
Milwaukee, Wisconsin.

negative seeds of dis-ease. Eventually, healing for the body came to me also as a result of the mental easement of worries and fears.

Truly, 'the joy of the Lord is full, and His mercy is from everlasting to everlasting!'

With much gratitude shall I always remember how my new life was channeled to me through this man who serves in such a unique way.

A like feeling of enthusiasm was expressed by a Paris physician:

> "I should like to say to my friends: 'you can write to Mr. Street.' For you are the most interesting of all the world. I know no other like you!"
>
> It would be a severe loss for the world if you should drop this work. . . ."

Noel Street among the Aborigines in Australia.

A Texas Welcome.

SECTION II

THE DEVELOPMENT OF POWER

Chapter 7

The Practice of Deep Meditation

The practice of deep meditation enables the consciousness of the seeker to become closely attuned to the power of Spirit. As we reach beyond the mind, we find that stillness which is termed the "Silence." By learning to still the mind himself, the seeker's consciousness can become absorbent to the voice of the Silence.

Awakening Psychic Powers

As the consciousness is changed, one's will becomes greatly influenced by the will of the Father — which is the purpose of deep meditation. The practice outlined in this chapter was conveyed to Noel Street fifteen years ago in a series of visions and is the method which he teaches in his classes today. It shows clearly how God as Light can be drawn closer to man's consciousness in a way which is not normally done, thus, enabling the aspirant to become one with Spirit Itself. Ultimately, the psychic powers are awakened.

The gifts of the Spirit which were mentioned earlier are said to be given to every man severally, and perhaps all of them could be available to persons who seek this meditative type of attunement with God.

Coin of Spirit Is Service

It is important that we bear in mind that there can
be no payment for these gifts. If "gifts," then they
are given freely, and we return the joy of these benefits through service to our Brother Man in love and
humility. At best, the person whose gifts are awakened
can only be a Servant of God, or a channel, or a
medium. Let us ask this question: Is a Christian really
developed if he has not awakened some of the gifts
which St. Paul mentions?

Man's Control Over the Elements

I have often heard Rev. Street speak on the superb
control which man has gained over the elements:
"He has constructed 'animals' out of minerals and
vegetables which can travel faster and longer distances
than those created through natural means. In this
way has he demonstrated his control over the element
of earth."

"Similarly, he has produced 'birds' which fly
longer distances than the natural ones.

"Man-made 'fishes' and 'flying fishes' are capable
of equalizing and sometimes surpassing the speed of
the live fishes themselves. This means of propulsion
(in most cases, propulsion energy) has been obtained
by the use of the fourth element — fire.

"And now we are treading on the threshold of
a new break-through into a more enlightened state
of consciousness by the meditative practice. Here,
man is learning to utilize his own Light by attuning
it to the Light of Spirit."

Your Wave Length of Light

George Fox's Society of Friends, the Quakers, were originally known as the Children of Light, and this quality has long been associated with the saints, rishis, and gurus. The artists have depicted such a person usually with a halo of light around the head.

It is interesting to know that each individual has his own particular wave-length in relation to the light. Sometimes it is a single color, but invariably the use of several intermingled colors can finally bring that state of unity between man's spirit and a heightened state of awareness.

As is known, light is broken down into the seven spectrum colors, ranging from red, which is the most dense of the lowest vibratory rate, to violet, being the highest color which the human eye can visualize. Of course, many other light vibrations exist beyond the range of the human's capacity to observe.

Your Own Sound Vibration

Each individual also has a sound vibration which commences as one 'quickens' in the embryonic state during pregnancy, at approximately 3½ months. This sound vibration is as individualized as our own fingerprints, our perfume, or our light. However, it can be developed if one wishes to bring about a state of greater attunement with God.

Even as the spectrum colors encompass the normal range of light vibration, there also exists a sound which envelops the whole range of the human vocab-

ulary. This three-lettered word, "AUM," covers
every language which has ever been utilized by Man
— past, present, and future. Even though it contains
only three letters, it occupies the entire vocal cavity
of the human mouth.

Sounding the "Aum"

Many readers will recognize the sound, although
the meaning is not well-known. If practiced during
meditation — either in silence or aloud — it will
strengthen the human vibratory wave length.

The word "AUM" normally is pronounced to
rhyme with "home." The letter "A" itself, when
sounded, commences at the back of the throat and
utilizes the local area to the roof of the mouth. The
letter "U" begins where the letter A finishes, namely,
the back of the mouth to the forward part of our
voice mechanism. The final "M" starts from the area
just behind the top piece to the closed lips of the
speaker.

The practice of this word is, in an auditory sense,
one complete and entire system of Yoga which is
practiced by some Indian people. However, we incorporate it in our meditation as a means of drawing
our consciousness into a more receptive state, so
that our inner ears become sensitive to the sound of
the Spirit of God.

Awakening Through Meditation

Any person with a normal intelligence can learn
deep meditation and can awaken the gifts of the

Chapter 3

The Origin of Disease

The healer soon recognizes that man not only possesses the physical body but is also heir to the very real emotional, mental, and spiritual compartments of his makeup. As he is constantly receiving impressions from the atmosphere around him, certain images gradually are built up in his mind which are either positive or negative. Very often a negative reaction to a situation is experienced by an individual and then ''forgotten'': however, psychologists and psychiatrists agree today that nothing is ever really erased from the memory but is stored in the subconscious layer of the mind.

Thus, we can see how inevitable pressures can build up within the bodies unless we learn how to control them. Very often, disease is the result of too great a pressure which manifests itself in the physical, more dense mechanism.

It is so easy for us to become a victim of this pressure. It exists all around us with our families, our ambitions, our work, and even our spiritual lives, all demanding personal attention. Quite naturally, we try to do our very best, but even the strongest body wilts under too great a pressure.

Achieving Balance

The Maori coat-of-arms represents a high degree of understanding, which is unmistakably reflected in the whole life style of the people. The sacred symbolism of this carving portrays a picture of a dismembered man, which is termed "Manaia." The meaning implies that unless man is balanced in his three aspects of body, mind, and spirit, he is in pieces and cannot be held together.

How can a balance be achieved in our lives so that we can control the disease? If an individual has the capacity to be honest, he will acknowledge the truth that "Only I can hurt myself." Or expressed another way: "Nothing can harm me unless I allow it to."

Therefore, to stop the inflow of negative forces into our lives, we can inject a control mechanism which will completely neutralize an adverse situation. This power is effected, first of all, by *recognizing* a problem, a hurtful act or word directed toward us, or anything that has been thought to be unfortunate. And then we can reverse its force from negative to positive by *thanking God for it!* When a soul has learned to express gratitude to the Father for the sorrows of life as well as for the joys, a new beginning is in store which can bring new joy, peace, good health, and happiness in abundance.

Pain is usually the better teacher for us earthlings, so that any obstacle we are required to overcome is an opportunity to grow spiritually. And if we can look at our experiences this way, we are offering ourselves better mental, spiritual, and physical health.

A Scientist's Experiment

Rev. Street once told me of an interesting experiment which was written about by a scientist who had never believed that a real, all-powerful, loving God existed.

Along with four other scientists in a large pathology laboratory, an experiment was executed in an attempt to measure the wave-length of the human brain; a channel of wave-lengths was discovered which was even more separable in identity than the fingerprints on an individual's hand.

The doctors wanted to know what took place in the brain at the moment of death and they chose two subjects.

The first patient was a woman who had cancer of the brain. This condition affected the balance of her body, but the alertness of her mind remained normal and she was exceptionally brilliant. The research hospital had informed her that she was on the verge of death, which she already knew.

The scientists who listened to the woman's dying response were a group of quite hardened men. They had devised a machine which had a scale wherein 500 points were calibrated from zero — negative to the left and positive to the right. They had previously registered on this instrument the power used by a 50 kilowatt broadcast station in sending a message around the world; the needle had registered nine points on the positive side.

As the woman lay dying, she began to pray asking that her Lord be merciful unto those persons who had spitefully used her. Then she re-affirmed her faith in God who was the Living Power. She thanked Him for His Power and the knowledge of His reality. And finally, she told Him how much she loved Him.

The scientists were so engrossed in this woman's prayer that tears were streaming down their faces. Suddenly, they heard a loud clicking sound on their forgotten instrument, and as they checked, the needle was registering a positive 500 and desperately trying to go higher!

By actual instrumentation they had recorded the brain wave of a woman, alone and dying, in communion with God — registering more than fifity-five times the power used by a 50 kilowatt broadcast station in sending a message around the world!

The second subject chosen for the experiment was a man whose brain had become atrophied to the point of death. He began to insult the nurse and the needle jerked back to the negative side. Then he cursed her with wild shrieks and quickly, the machine needle clicked against the 500 negative post.

In conclusion, the scientists were quite moved by the human individual's ability to use his power either positively or negatively in such varying degrees.

If we should choose to use our own powers positively, think how greatly our lives would be enhanced by the Spirit of love and the power of healing for others, as well as for ourselves.

The Birth of Spiritual Healing

In moments of extreme anguish we cry to that infinite power beyond ourselves for help. In this manner was spiritual healing born, probably around 250,000 years ago when man, recognizing the divine life within himself, began to bury his dead.

Thus, we can generalize that someone has sent out a distress signal when he seeks relief from pain or suffering. This key in the picture of spiritual healing lies in the desire of the person who truly wants to get well.

If we believe in herbs and their curative powers, would not we then contact the herbalist for treatment? However, because man is a creature with mind, emotions, body, and spirit, he may find that herbs or medications are limited in relieving his illness. Hence, he may ultimately seek aid from God by contactng his priest or spiritual healer who acts as a channel for this God-Force.

Man has obtained balm for his suffering in like manner for many thousands of years. The gift of healing is one of nine gifts of the Spirit which Saint Paul mentions in I Corinthians, 12. In looking closer, we find the list increased: WISDOM, KNOWLEDGE, FAITH, HEALING, MIRACLES, PROPHECY, DISCERNMENT OF SPIRITS, SPEAKING IN TONGUES, AND THE INTERPRETATION OF TONGUES.

It is most apparent to all open-minded truth seekers today that religion is changing from blind faith to personal involvement in the power of God's Spirit. The ancient gifts of the Spirit are truly recognized and gratefully received by our generation, while knowledge of the mysteries is no longer solely in the keeping of church officers,

The leaning toward this supremely natural way of healing via the Spirit which is within man and external to him, often has sent forth an eagerness to seek spiritual healing in preference to drugs, tranquilizing or pain killing remedies, surgery or psychoanalysis.

"My Cup Runneth Over"

Recently, while in San Jose, California on a national tour a woman went to Rev. Street for a healing treatment. She came in great pain because of an internal growth, and surgery had been recommended by her physician. However, sensing that she could be helped through other means, the doctor suggested that she visit Rev. Street.

Clairvoyantly, an obstruction was sensed in her descending colon, and during the treatment he felt exceptionally strong psychic power being conveyed through his hands to her painful abdomen.

"I felt something move!" she exclaimed afterwards.

On seeing her again in a few days, the pain had vanished, and she reported that she felt much better.

To a full time healer, such incidents are not unusual. Seeing a patient respond favorably is relatively commonplace, but the letter which was received from the lady a month later makes warm reading:

"My cup runneth over with joy! Now I know the meaning of it. Get out your casebook, dear friend, and mark 'O.K.' beside my name. The tumor in the descending colon is gone! I shall never forget the physician's voice as he read the X-ray report to me over the phone. There was excitement, surprise and delight, but he was completely mystified. In just three weeks a six-inch long tumor dissolved!

I have been healed spiritually and physically by God — coming through a very wonderful person who was a channel for this power."

Even as we sense the happiness and gratitude which this woman expresses for having been able to bypass the surgery, we wonder how many other patients could avoid operations if they sought help from spiritual healers who are quietly working today, either in their churches or privately.

Again, illness is the result of pressure. A developed healer can lift that pressure and in many cases is able to describe what has caused it to occur.

Any overwork results in pressure. Whether the strain be in our emotional, mental, or spiritual body, the breakdown will manifest in the physical vehicle sooner or later.

It is a joy to see more men who are in the medical profession using their spiritual powers to bring relief from suffering. Patients are only too pleased to find that by right eating, right thinking, right breathing and right living they can enjoy life as never before.

A Healer in Disguise

One of the first friends whom the Streets made in America was a woman named Mary from the East Coast. Being mother of seven children as well as wife to a brilliant physicist, she still finds the extra energy to give lectures on health and right diet.

Because Mary is so obviously glowing with good health and happiness herself, I found it difficult to picture her as she was said to be a few years back. Apparently, she suffered from a tremendous metabolic dysfunction in her body, which ultimately left her tired, emotionally unstable, and childless.

Seeking help from the doctors, they admitted that they did not have enough knowledge of the subject to help her at that time. So the young woman went on her way, experimenting with diet and nutrition, determined to find a solution herself. ''I was truly guided by Spirit in finding help for this disease. Believe me, when I first started out, I was a wreck — physically and mentally!'' she recounts.

The results of her search for better health have certainly paid off, with her excellent mothering of seven children (which, incidentally, followed!), and in the authority which she has become in the field of nutrition. ''Compared to those years in college and early married life, I am quite different now; I can go eighteen hours a day and still have energy to spare!'' she says.

And her efforts especially show in her gardening project, as she tends a half-acre plot herself and does all the canning of vegetables and fruits in order to provide a near perfect diet for her beloved family.

This year, Mary appeared on several hour-long television programs, telling other families how they, too, can achieve better health through right nutrition. Indeed, her own life is an example of good health — physically, mentally, and spiritually, so that her message is channeled to others in the most effective manner. In a true sense, she herself is a healer of disease.

Chapter 4

The Scope of Emotional Healing

Have you ever wondered how the emotional body is connected to the physical? If one could see the less dense molecular structure of the emotional body, he would know that the two are connected by a third etheric body made of normally invisible particles. Because such close association does exist among the bodies of this intricately designed system, it is easy to understand how an imbalance in one could quite readily affect the others.

Since the bodies interact so closely, one would find it difficult to say that all physical ills could not in some measure be traced back to some pressure in the highly charged emotional vehicle of the patient.

Healing Through Understanding

On one occasion the wife of the Managing Director of a large manufacturing plant, who had received healing treatment from Rev. Street, came again, bringing the maid who scrubbed floors in her husband's office. The executive's wife had seen the woman's legs covered in red blotches, and taking pity on her, brought her for healing. When they arrived, one in furs and the other in an old wrap, Rev. Street was delighted to see that the old charwoman was a very spiritually developed soul, although of humble speech and poor circumstances.

The two women sat down for the healing to begin, and the healer asked the charwoman if she cared to offer a prayer of blessing. Until this time, they had only spoken in greeting, and Rev. Street again was pleased to hear the beautiful utterance which came from the poor body. The Light truly shone through her as she prayed not for herself, but for the healer and the kind person who had brought her.

The patient's legs and back were almost raw with the skin disorder, which was caused from an emotional strain on her for many years. She had acted as babysitter, banker, general servant, and friend-in-need to all her relatives, until finally the pressure became too much for her and manifested itself in the physical through the wretched sores on her body.

It was explained to her that her total unselfishness to family and friends had, in fact, increased the selfishness of all those persons around her. So the solution was to 'put her foot down' on all unnecessary requests and to discontinue part of the services which had ultimately caused her this pressure.

She took this advice, and very quickly her rash began to heal and disappear. Considering the fact that her severe affliction was practically bleeding when she came, a very wonderful healing was experienced.

"The disease is incurable . . ."

Thoughts are things, and energy follows thought. Hence, when a patient is handed the frequent decree, "The disease is incurable — you must learn to live with it,'' the negative thought contained therein is similar to being handed the tools and materials to construct a coffin to size. However, in most cases, if the approach could be re-directed toward undestanding *why* a dysfunction has occurred, then more people would recover, even from the myriad ''incurables.''

Freedom Through Right Thinking

Another patient had been receiving treatment at a hospital in Leicester Square, London, for the period of twelve months in an attempt to control a bright red rash extending from below her eyes and covering half her cheeks. At last, the woman sought help through spiritual healing.

As she sat before Rev. Street for the first time, psychically he viewed a will and questioned if she had experienced any difficulty over such a legal matter. She did not reply for a few minutes, then, reluctantly she admitted that she and her sister had not communicated for more than twenty years due to a dispute over a will.

Realizing the reason for the skin disorder, the healer asked her if she would make the effort to get in touch with the sister and attempt to restore the relationship, even as he aided the return of the life force to her cheeks.

On seeing her the following week, the patient had heard from her sister and they were again friends. Within six weeks there was no sign of a skin blemish, and the rash has not since reappeared.

Later a letter came expressing her joy:

". . .For myself, my healing (emotional) is complete,
and I can smile to think how foolish I have been, hugging
this resentment all these years. It seemed that I would
never be able to loose it and let go . . . I am so
glad to be free!"

Using Psychic Power to Diagnose

As Rev. Street began his healing ministry, he was
trained in the use of color during meditation. From
the beginning of this practice, his psychic power
continually unfolded so that while he was interview-
ing a patient, he could close his eyes and see mental
pictures which aided him in diagnosis.

As certain pictures appeared he was often required
to seek an explanation for what he saw, and ultimately, he would discover the reason for a particular
distress.

As he has developed this faculty to help many
people, the cause of illness is often relayed to him in
this manner, involving inherent pressures in the emotional as well as the physical body. Many people
who least expect it are exhibiting discomfort which
stems from a deep emotional barb in their subconscious of which they are not even aware. And it is
the healer's desire to uncover this painful emotional
area so that the patient can experience the full measure of radiant health through healing power.

A lovely lady heard of Rev. Street's work and
came with a certain medical complaint which had
slowly developed over a six-month period but was
rapidly becoming worse. Twice she had been hospital-

ized and the doctors could not pinpoint or agree upon a definite diagnosis beyond a certain chemical imbalance which was found.

When she came for treatment, a picture was shown of her psychically wherein Rev. Street viewed her as a large tree entwined by three vines which were choking and draining the life force from her. On each vine was portrayed the face of a family member.

As the meaning of these particular details was interpreted, the patient quickly recognized the need to become free from certain family ties which had bound her by demands on her time, as well as engaged a hold on the expression of her spiritual nature.

Because she needed more freedom in her life in several respects, certain adjustments were made which eventually allowed a complete recovery in the physical body. Again, her energy and enthusiasm speaks of the deep love with which this vibrant woman joyously serves Spirit.

Projecting the Christ Light

How easily and unexpectedly we sometimes become shackled by situations around us. Often we find that our home life is one of the most vulnerable pressure points.

Recently, a young mother came to the healing temple and requested treatment for herself and her son. Quickly, Rev. Street was able to assess a situation in her life which she found difficult to face. Gently he asked: ''Is there something in your home which you have found to be less painful if just ig-

nored?'' Immediately tears began to well up and flow
as she explained, ''Oh, yes, it's something that I've
wanted to talk to you about!''

And with this beginning, the patient explained
that her divorced father had been quite disgruntled
for several years and had continually made unreasonable demands on the entire family. Any efforts
to please him were never satisfying to him, and his
constant accusations inferred that no one cared
whether he lived or died.

Finally, the family was so worn down by this
man's grumbling, that they were forced to sever the
relationship for their own sake. But there was still the
emotional tie and resultant pressure which was expressing itself through illness in the family.

Through counseling, the woman was able to see
that her father was quite enjoying the control and
power which he held over family members through
his childish demands, and that in order to relieve the
emotional pressure on herself, adjustments could be
made.

First, she could begin to live more closely attuned
to the spiritual side of her nature by *thanking God*
for this experience. This attitude of gratitude is a sure
antidote for a feeling of depression.

Next, she was told that she could send a blessing
by projecting a white cross above her father's head
whenever she thought of him, the benefit being a direct
association of the Christ-love between herself and
him. This method of acknowledging and uplifting the
Christ Consciousness in another person is a sure
way of clearing the subconscious of any past emotional debris.

Finally, the patient was advised to go to the man and let him know in a very loving but *firm* way that he was welcome in their home. However, they no longer intended to cater to his irrational whims, which had disrupted the entire family unit.

In effect, this patient's healing came through learning to look at life more objectively, ultimately detaching herself a bit from the emotional aspect of life and seeking to live more fully in the spiritual dimension.

After a few weeks, a letter came from the woman expressing her gratitude for Rev. Street's work, and saying:

> "A powerful change has occurred recently, benefiting the entire family. Through your guidance the closed door has opened, and my father and I have been reconciled. The power is still working . . . ."

It is obvious to us all that even though we may be treated for an illness and become better, no permanent change can be brought about unless we eventually remove the cause of the pressure. Otherwise, we will be forced to seek help continually from the medical doctors, chiropractors, or healers who serve us. Thus, understanding the "why" of our ills is essentially linked to the "how" of treatment.

Healing the Emotions

Quite often a patient will come to the Healing Sanctuary who has an emotional problem which has not necessarily caused a gross physical reaction in the body. However, one could suspect a physical symptom to occur eventually, should the condition remain uncorrected. Therefore, Rev. Street uses the same method for diagnosis as was described earlier.

A young Maori nurse of twenty-six who had been nursing in a psychiatric hospital went to see Rev. Street. Being of an unusually sensitive nature, she had become disturbed by the conditions around her and had herself found the work extremely depressing to her health. This situation, coupled with the burden of two fractious children, had sent her temporarily off balance and she finally became a patient herself.

Her mother explained that the pressures of work and the children had drained her daughter of all vitality. A need existed to ease this burden and let the God-Force take over in her life.

Rev. Street found that the mother had neglected to tell her of the ancient Maori custom of blessing children at birth. In doing this, she was able to divest herself of the soulic responsibility of the children, which eased her lot considerably. One could say this act had a deep subconscious effect on the woman, so that she also began to see the suffering of her patients in a more objective light. Within a few weeks, she was well and able to take over the role of housewife and mother once more.

In my own experience also have I seen many people restored to health in a miraculous way. One particular friend shall I always remember who became quite ill through gross confusions and personal worries in her life. Not knowing how to handle these

harassments of the mind, the poor girl began to se-
date herself with a profusion of drugs, tranquilizers,
and anti-depressants of every description. It was in
this state that I first met her, and my heart was
moved with a great sympathy for her and a desire
to befriend her.

Several months after our first introduction, I began to feel a tremendous urge to contact her. On
arriving at her house, her mother and sister came to
the door looking quite distraught and explained that
she had attempted suicide.

"The doctors don't have much hope, because she
is still unconscious and hasn't responded," said her
mother who was a registered nurse.

Quite jarred by the news, I went home and found
that I really did not know how to pray for her. So
I mumbled some prayers for her soul and sent a
flood of love to her spirit. Presently, I opened the
Bible in a semi-aware state myself, and the words
from Psalms fairly lunged at me from the page: "I
SHALL NOT DIE, BUT LIVE, AND DECLARE
THE WORKS OF THE LORD!"

Amazed at this message, I read it again and again,
receiving a tremendous comfort and realization that
the girl would not only live but would find herself
in a fully identified way with Spirit.

The next day news came that she had regained
consciousness and would be fine. Of course, I knew
that her emotional healing would take more time,
and as I look back now after three years, I can
readily see the power of Spirit working in her life
through the help of doctors, a minister friend, and
many others who have shared similar experiences,

strength, and hope. Still struggling and still growing, her last letter quite lovingly read:

    "I am learning to trust and have faith that even though I can't possibly see the end-result of this experience I'm still an 'OK' person. I know that there is meaning for my little life, and it will reveal itself more and more with time."

Quite a lovely interlude, I must say, for a beautiful soul who has left behind the old way and is ever seeking the Higher Experience in her life — found through the Spirit of Healing in our world.

Chapter 5

Working with Animals and Children

Generally, children and animals make wonderful patients, for no barriers exist in their minds.

Love for All Creation

In some countries spiritual healers do not treat animals believing the animal kingdom to be a lower level of life which will inevitably lower their healing standards. Others heal animals exclusively.

As in all types of healing, we find sympathy to be the motivating factor in bringing ease to suffering. Usually the animal healer is the type of person whose love envelops all of creation but who has a particular magnetism towards animals.

In his healing work, Rev. Street has treated those few animals which he has just happened upon. One such case included an old budgerigar named Peter who was dying. The little bird meant a lot to the elderly woman who owned it, and the vet had blamed its sickness on old age. Hunched over in the bottom of the cage the bird remained with its food untouched.

As Rev. Street closed his eyes, he was shown a small portion of blocked intestine The suggestion for curing the animal entailed placing a sheet of blotting paper on the floor of the cage and sprinkling several drops of paraffin thereon. Furthermore, the bird's seed was soaked overnight in a solution of Epsom Salts.

Seeing her a few weeks later, the lady was much happier and joyfully explained that Peter had made a complete recovery!

Because the healer himself loves birds, he, on one occasion, bought a mixed lot of hens varying in age and breed. Among them was a small chicken, about two months old, with an unfortunate malady of which the other birds took advantage. "Blindie," as the Street family came to call her, had a white film over one eye which blocked the vision on that side, and the other chickens pecked her if she got too near the feed trough.

Because her life was so miserable, Rev. Street pitied the poor bird and separated her from the rest of the flock. Each day, at regular intervals, he treated the bad eye with spiritual healing. Within a week, the white patch receded to the back of the eye permitting normal frontal vision and 80% total vision all around.

The other birds quickly recognized a change and accepted her, for now she could peck them back as easily as they pecked her. "Blindie" was a favorite pet around the household, as she became quite tame and would run to greet anyone who passed by.

Transmigration from Animal to Human

Sometimes the meaning of pain has its place in our lives whether the suffering involves the animal or the human level of experience.

Several months ago, a friend from New Zealand wrote of an incident with her pet.

"The other morning I was shown the meaning of transmigration. Until then, I sat on the fence with this idea, neither holding nor rejecting a definite patent as to the validity of this thought.

Our dog, Cindy, had suffered agony from eczema for many months, and I should have had her put to sleep but something stopped me. Perhaps it was the fact that Swami R. in one of his lectures had told a story about three people meeting an animal in pain: the first one helped it all he could; the next one shot it to put it out of its misery; and the third man, a sage, looked at it smiling and walked on, understanding that this experience had to be endured for the creature's own evolvement.

In meditation I asked for guidance in knowing what to do about the pet, and the next day I was shown a remarkable thing! I saw Cindy in her poor body and felt her nipping me as if to hurry me along and get it done; she was anxious to go on. Then I saw her higher body leaping from the old, full of vibrant health, intelligence, and love. Finally, it was shown to me how she would eventually reincarnate into a male form — a boy with shoulder-length hair who exuded an aura of love — and to me came the name 'Bill Prussett.'

The whole experience was quite fascinating, and immediately I arranged to have the animal put to sleep. The next day Cindy was in a state of heightened consciousness and seemed to be having spiritual experiences. She knew, also. We took her and she went gladly — too gladly — staying close to me, but not quite in this world. I patted her, spoke to her softly until it was all over. Never have I seen a happier, more peaceful passing. Then I went out to the car and bawled my eyes out.''

Releasing Prejudice to Receive Spirit

Because we are often so steeped in preconceived ideas, we remain barred from certain opportunities which could enhance our lives. This blockage has its effect in our spiritual lives and quite aptly applies when related to healing.

The Maori people are gifted with quite a lovely power for healing and they know of many ways in which this power can be brought down to ease suffering. These people are also aware of the spiritual law that says this knowledge must be shared with others, lest they lose the power themselves.

One day, the child of a white New Zealand couple was outside playing while his parents were away for a short while. Somehow, the boy got a bone lodged in his throat and began to gasp for air. Luckily, some Maori people came upon him and discovered his plight. Quickly, realizing the necessity for speed, one of the old Maori tribesmen began using a healing incantation, and immediately, the child's life was saved as the object was loosed and freed from his throat.

Grateful for the aid which his neighbors had rendered, he rushed home to wait for his parents and tell them what had happened.

With utter amazement, the Maoris soon found the parents on their doorstep — not with gratitude for saving the child but with airy indignation for using "superstitious rite."

"Don't you ever put your hands on our son again!"'came the decree!

Because of the ingrained prejudice against a different race who had passed down many traditions from generation to generation, they failed to hold any understanding nor even any gratitude for the child's survival. Fortunately, the boy was not possessed by the same attitudes of his parents, and the Maoris had served him as their Brother.

Maori Medicine

The same vein of feeling toward the 'primitives' is reflected in a similar story of a Maori child whose grandmother used ancient tribal wisdom and psychic healing to restore him to health.

Having injured his foot, Piri's body had stored up an infection which had left him hysterical with fever. Quickly, Granny employed her age old bush cure of wrapping the limb with a leaf poultice which had been boiled in a certain herbal solution. Along with this cure, she applied the power of psychic healing which came from her father before her.

As the child finally awoke to his normal consciousness, Granny smiled and stooped to place her cool hand on his little forehead. The afternoon sun lay in long shafts across his bed, as the child glanced down at the fat parcel around his foot.

"Don't worry, little one. Granny has brought you medicine from the bush. Soon you will be quite well again, but first we must sleep. Your Granny is very tired."

Soon a quaint 'pakeha' woman appeared at the door of the hut, ready to impose the 'white' medicine on the natives.

"A nurse has been called for the child," came the neighbor's announcement as she gazed around the room to see the shiny black stove and scrubbed white table top.

When the nurse arrived, she found the child's temperature to be normal. "Your medicine must be very good; you must tell us how to use it."

The grandmother was silent for a long time before answering. "No, Maori medicine is best used by the old people" was her soft answer.

The next day Piri was outside playing again, his foot almost completely well.

Of course, the Maori people are not the sole possessors of such ancient healing arts. Similar knowledge, for example, has been preserved in the heritage of the Indians and the Eskimos. Unfortunately, the demands of sophistication which an "evolved" society such as our own has placed upon us, are often quick to cloud such attunement with Spirit by a single clinical approach.

Children and animals, however, continue to respond more readily to spiritual healing with their

simple trust, for they are not yet clothed in the dis-
advantages of a narrowed thinking. Thus, they are
more open to the power of Spirit in their lives, whatever form it may take.

Jumping the Big Ones!

A child is usually as unconcerned with the "how"
of healing as he is with the person before him wearing
the white coat. All that matters to a child is getting
well so that he can go out and play once more.

A young boy of five was brought to the Healing
Sanctuary with an extreme case of asthma. He dis-
played a great difficulty in breathing, and after the
boy was checked and treated, Rev. Street made certain recommendations to be used during the day.

Within three weeks, the child showed remarkable
improvement and he was happy to return for further
treatment. Walking to the Sanctuary with his mother,
he was stamping out the last few blocks with new
enthusiasm.

"Gee, I love to go to see Rev. Street."

"Why?" the mother queried.

"Because on the way I can jump over that big
hole in the road, and on the way back I can jump
over it again!" was the reply.

Such is the joy of children in their simplicity of
expression.

The Joy of Light

Another child was brought for treatment, who had
a congenital birth defect. Within one eye was a de-

tached retina, but the doctors had refused to operate due to the fact that he was too young for this kind of surgery.

Rev. Street treated him on three occasions, and quite readily the eye responded to healing, restoring vision completely. As the lad sat before him on the last visit, he began to laugh aloud. The whole occurrence had suddenly struck him as being funny, because "the *other* man said I would never be able to see!"

Last year Rev. Street witnessed two marvelous demonstrations of spiritual healing. A boy of eight and a girl of fifteen were seeing with their eyes for the first time after he was used as a channel to heal their blindness. The girl especially grew in beauty as the sight returned to her eyes.

A healer's life is peopled with many awesome experiences, but perhaps one of the greatest joys is having a child speak of improvement. Furthermore, it is a humbling and joyous experience to realize that someone who has his whole life ahead of him has been made well.

Chapter 6
Healing and Reincarnation

A short while after Noel Street began his healing ministry in London, a very strange thing occurred. A woman came for an appointment, as she was experiencing severe emotional distress. For some unknown reason, extreme panic would overtake her when she was in a crowd and someone had to accompany her whenever she went out in public. In fact, this particular problem had always disturbed her, so she finally went to the Clinic seeking aid.

The healer had prayed hard that he might be used to help this unfortunate woman, and as she sat before him, she asked: "Rev. Street, do you think this fear could be a carry-forward from another life?"

Quite taken aback by this question, he had never really pondered such a thought. Closing his eyes and asking a prayer of guidance from Spirit, he suddenly began to see flashes of a past life when she was a resident in Rome. Caught in a seething crowd of spectators at a Roman game, the reason for the present-day fear was quickly established as he described this scene to her. Immediately, she exclaimed with an affirmative 'Ah, yes!''

With great amazement, he was as surprised as his patient over this incident, for until that time he had never been able to view past lives. Eventually, this gift was to enhance his healing ministry greatly, as the ability of seeing into the past became more developed.

Of course, this gift did not present itself full-blown in the beginning. Instead, the healer simply noticed that gradually as people sought his advice and help with certain problems, the scenes of their past lives flashed more frequently before his mind's eye.

A New Gauge for Evaluation

Very quickly, this man was able to evaluate disease and difficulty in a new light. In most instances, he found identical problems appearing in the patients' current lives as had beset them in the past. Furthermore, certain karmic tendencies seemed to occur *as a result of* past happenings, and with this knowledge came a more far-reaching healing ministry in every way.

As one studies the doctrine of reincarnation, he can see how the psyche can become overcrowded and disturbed from the pressures that have accumulated and then been passed on from one life to another. As most people know, excessive worry and stress can easily be regarded as an illness in itself. Ultimately, as we move away from control and balance in our lives, for whatever reason, inevitably we move toward a state wherein we lack harmony. This dis-ease within ourselves must be corrected or we suffer.

Recently, a good friend of the Streets wrote from New Zealand saying that she was experiencing some difficulty with her 93-year-old mother.

"Mother is quite reluctant to face the prospect of death," writes Lucy. "Not only does she fail to believe in reincarnation, but neither can she bring herself to expect life after death. Several times I've had her convinced of survival, but she's so old she keeps forgetting!"

Understanding His Child's Fear

As Rev. Street developed in the field of reincarnation tracings, he found a certain problem within his own family which he suspected might be relative to an experience from a past life.

One of his daughters showed an abnormal aversion to fire in that when she entered a room which had a heater or fireplace burning, she would immediately attempt to extinguish the blaze or uplift the grate. Furthermore, the sound of a passing fire engine was so frightening to her that she would always respond: "What is *that*? It must be a police wagon!" Any avoidance of the idea that it was a fire truck was fully and tenaciously explained away by the fearful child.

As her father "read" some of her past lives, he readily understood the source of the present-day trouble. In a recent life, she had been trapped in an attic on the top story of a burning building. Unable to escape, she had succumbed to the blaze and, as might be expected, had carried forward into the present life a particularly strong fear of fire.

To aid the child in overcoming the traumatic effect of the accident on her subconscious mind, a

certain technique was used to treat her, and immediately she responded favorably.

Argument for Viewing Past Lives

Many people who believe in reincarnation argue
that knowing one's past lives is of no value. They
say, "That's all in the past. I'm only concerned about
living this life!" or perhaps, "I have all I can manage
with *this* life!"

However, if they truly understood that each life
is not a separate unrelated happening but a continual
flow of character traits, situations, and karmic patterns set up to be overcome, a new light of understanding would penetrate their minds and offer to
withdraw pressure instead of adding a burden.

A life in physical form bears for each of us the
opportunity to learn those lessons which only a physical existence can teach. The explanation of reincarnation can be likened to school; life is the schoolroom
where we learn lessons, and if we fail to learn certain ones, we must return again and again until our
purpose of spiritual progress and understanding
has been achieved. A person ordinarily has many
lives, both male and female, until a heightened state
of consciousness is reached.

With the long-range view of reincarnation before
us, we can begin to see the justice in life, the true
meaning of the equality of birth, and the "law of
reaction" in operation. No longer must one struggle
with life's imponderables, of which there are so
many; instead, a true structure for living is perceived,

as a person learns of the spiritual laws under which he lives. This understanding can help speed up his spiritual progress on the pathway of life.

Furthermore, most people who seek knowledge of their past lives for the sake of spiritual guidance usually receive abundant light on their individual pathways.

A Wife's Karma

A close friend of mine married a man who later became an alcoholic. In trying to raise their small children and deal with the inherent problems in this relationship, she experienced a great deal of heartache and woe. At one point she was tempted to leave her husband because of the pressures which were upon her. However, putting her Spiritual will to work, she eventually overcame the difficulties of the physical plane by living more within the spiritual realm.

Of course, this process took time, for thought patterns which have been set up over a period of years are not changed in a week. But through living one day at a time, this woman was able to change herself and her own thinking to the point of completely changing the direction of her whole life.

Her husband, along with the children, responded quite well to the new aura of love and peace which was poured out from Spirit and channeled through this woman. Fifteen years later, the family has become a signpost of great encouragement as they extend much love and understanding toward people who are having similar emotional problems which they themselves experienced in earlier years.

About a year ago, this woman was privileged
to have a reincarnation reading of her past lives by
Rev. Street, who had no knowledge of her present
life whatsoever.

One of the first lives which he viewed for her explained the reason for her present karma. She had
been born in France in the 18th century and had
sought extremes for her happiness. Finally, in marriage she chose a man who later became addicted to
alcohol; throughout the remainder of her life she had
abhorred this habit and illness in him and had left
him after several years of marriage. Never did she
use the power of her spiritual nature to help understand or ease the karma under which they lived.

As a result of failing to overcome this problem
which a physical life had set before her, she was required to return to a similar situation and experience
it again as an opportunity to use her Spiritual will.
As was in evidence by the events of her present life,
this woman had not only worked out her karma but
used the experience to serve her Brother Man! Such
is the message of rebirth — not only physically, but
spiritually as well.

This example is only one of many which is
evidence of karmic patterns set up and brought into
the present life.

Unusual Demonstrations on Radio and Television

One distinguishing mark of Rev. Street's ministry is that he is probably the only living man who
has ever publicly demonstrated on radio and television his remarkable ability of looking backwards

in time. His television debut in America was on the ''fearsome'' Joe Pyne Show. Since then, he has appeared hundreds of times over public media and thrilled audiences in many parts of the world.

As people have seen and heard of this unusual gift, whole families have gone to him for reincarnation readings, often taking infants for the purpose of vocational guidance.

One such family to seek the benefits of his ability to trace past lives was the physicist and his wife mentioned earlier who have seven children. Seeking this knowledge of past lives in relation to the present has been an immeasurable aid to each family member. As the oldest daughter said, ''The readings for our family were of great help in directing us toward suitable vocations, as well as uncovering certain problems which had not been explainable. Generally, we were all able to understand our individual karma, and it was a thrilling experience for the whole family!''

Each week brings many letters to Rev. Street concerning the fact that reincarnation readings have real value in increasing understanding and easing difficult circumstances.

One such letter came from Australia:

''Dear Rev. Street,

Thank you for an excellent reading. This is really a slum clearance project, my past being slums, and *you,* the one enabling me to see how an area must be levelled for new foundations to be laid; when this is done, I shall eventually be of use to the right forces, so you are doing much more than merely pointing out landmarks to a tourist . . . .''

Another gentlemen from South Africa writes expressing his gratitude in understanding himself better:

"Dear Sir,

The survey of my past lives, which you have drawn up for me, was delivered at my home on Christmas Eve.
Let me say quite plainly that it was the most wonderful Christmas present I have ever received. . . .You are quite right regarding the negative qualities in my past, because some of them are still my weaknesses in this life, but now I have the courage to try and overcome them with God's help.
I wish to thank you a thousand times for what I consider a most accurate and fascinating revelation!"

These letters are only two examples of cases wherein reincarnation readings have given the added impetus of correcting those personal imperfections which block spiritual progress.

Particularly am I grateful for this strong arm of Noel Street's outreach, for it was with his guidance through the help of a reading that I received healing for both the mind and body.

Finding myself quite distraught over a lack of satisfying answers which various philosophies and religions had handed me, I began to tell a close friend of the turmoil which was constantly erupting within me. Perhaps I had reached a new plateau of readiness, for Spirit directed me at that moment into an unfamiliar area of thought and experience.

As the friend listened, he recognized my queries as being directly related to the belief in reincarnation, in which he himself was firmly grounded. As he explained the necessity of returning again and again to the earth plane in order to benefit from certain experiences for our learning, my heart began to pound ecstatically!

It seemed that all the fears of so many years dropped from me, and for the first time in this life was I free and able to soar, to feel real joy, and to replace an overwhelming fear of God with true reverence, love and adoration!

For me, this discovery was a prelude to the joyous strain of my soul: "Ye shall know the truth, and truth will make you free!"

And never has this new-found song lessened in its hold upon my heart. It has served to illumine my pathway more each day, offering a new depth of meaning in the awareness that we are all God's children, and that "all His sons will one day reach His feet, however far they stray!" A lost soul is an impossibility.

Music to My Ears

Within a week Spirit led me further in this new adventure. I dropped in unexpectedly to visit a friend named Mary Jane, and she was unusually excited that day.

"I've got something to tell you!" she spouted out. And quickly she brought out a tape recording.

Without giving me time for questions, she went on about ". . . a man who can look backward . . . Noel Street! . . . and a reincarnation reading. . . .

Slowly, I began to piece the words together and understood that a man named Noel Street in New

York had traced back some of her past lives. Having a growing belief in continuous incarnations myself, I was intrigued by the notion that anyone could possibly possess such a faculty of looking backwards in time. So I asked her if we could listen to the tape together.

Sitting down and hardly knowing what to expect, I strained my ears, determined to hear every word that the 'voice' repeated. As the tracing began, Rev. Street was seeing my friend in 'what was your most recent life. . . . You lived in Germany in the 19th century . . . a female who loved music and dancing. . .''

With those words out, a strange song from a music box began to play in the room where the two of us sat, and our attention was immediately jerked back in wonder and surprise!

"Where is that music coming from?'' we both queried simultaneously! Switching off the recorder, Mary Jane spotted a little music box on the dresser which had somehow been released, even though the lid had not been lifted; and it was playing a song — a *German* melody, in fact!

Attempting to stop the sound, she found that the box was mysteriously jammed and had to run down before it would cut off.

Coincidence? Perhaps. But it was strange that the box had never before — or has since — jammed. Whatever the explanation one may apply, I must add that the remainder of Mary Jane's reading held great interest for me. And somehow I left that day with a deeper conviction in the validity of reincarnation.

Within a week, I had received a tracing of my own lives from Rev. Street and was amazed at the unmistakable resembling patterns which flowed from the account of the past into my present life.

It can never be emphasized enough that one will receive from a reading no more and no less than what he asks. When one desires this help from Rev. Street solely out of curiosity about the past, no doubt he will be dealt no more than a review of geographical locations, dates, cultures, and such details of by-gone experiences.

While on the last tour across the country, the Street caravan had halted temporarily in a large city. As is usually the case, we found that the sponsors for the public meetings had completely booked the appointment time prior to our arrival.

As one woman sat patiently waiting for an 'Akashic Life Reading,' I noticed on the application form that she had stated her reason for wanting the tracing to be 'curiosity.' I explained that Rev. Street did not trace past lives for that purpose — he required a more solid approach, such as understanding karma.

As quickly as I had challenged her motive, she retorted with equal speed: "Oh, well, that's what I'm curious about — my karma!" Needless to say, she got her reading and we got a good laugh!

Quite different from her light approach, I sought through my reading to know the purpose of my life — a question which desperately gnawed on me from the inside. And inevitably the understanding and direction came, accompanied by an inherent healing of the mind. And from that guidepost onward in my journeying, I have never been required to return to the old way of thinking that had cultured and grown

Noel on television.

Noel speaking on Rebirth to a capacity audience in
Milwaukee, Wisconsin.

negative seeds of dis-ease. Eventually, healing for the body came to me also as a result of the mental easement of worries and fears.

Truly, 'the joy of the Lord is full, and His mercy is from everlasting to everlasting!'

With much gratitude shall I always remember how my new life was channeled to me through this man who serves in such a unique way.

A like feeling of enthusiasm was expressed by a Paris physician:

"I should like to say to my friends: 'you can write to Mr. Street.' For you are the most interesting of all the world. I know no other like you!"

It would be a severe loss for the world if you should drop this work. . . ."

Noel Street among the Aborigines in Australia.

A Texas Welcome.

SECTION II

THE DEVELOPMENT OF POWER

Chapter 7

The Practice of Deep Meditation

The practice of deep meditation enables the consciousness of the seeker to become closely attuned to the power of Spirit. As we reach beyond the mind, we find that stillness which is termed the "Silence." By learning to still the mind himself, the seeker's consciousness can become absorbent to the voice of the Silence.

Awakening Psychic Powers

As the consciousness is changed, one's will becomes greatly influenced by the will of the Father — which is the purpose of deep meditation. The practice outlined in this chapter was conveyed to Noel Street fifteen years ago in a series of visions and is the method which he teaches in his classes today. It shows clearly how God as Light can be drawn closer to man's consciousness in a way which is not normally done, thus, enabling the aspirant to become one with Spirit Itself. Ultimately, the psychic powers are awakened.

The gifts of the Spirit which were mentioned earlier are said to be given to every man severally, and perhaps all of them could be available to persons who seek this meditative type of attunement with God.

Coin of Spirit Is Service

It is important that we bear in mind that there can
be no payment for these gifts. If "gifts," then they
are given freely, and we return the joy of these benefits through service to our Brother Man in love and
humility. At best, the person whose gifts are awakened
can only be a Servant of God, or a channel, or a
medium. Let us ask this question: Is a Christian really
developed if he has not awakened some of the gifts
which St. Paul mentions?

Man's Control Over the Elements

I have often heard Rev. Street speak on the superb
control which man has gained over the elements:
"He has constructed 'animals' out of minerals and
vegetables which can travel faster and longer distances
than those created through natural means. In this
way has he demonstrated his control over the element
of earth."

"Similarly, he has produced 'birds' which fly
longer distances than the natural ones.

"Man-made 'fishes' and 'flying fishes' are capable
of equalizing and sometimes surpassing the speed of
the live fishes themselves. This means of propulsion
(in most cases, propulsion energy) has been obtained
by the use of the fourth element — fire.

"And now we are treading on the threshold of
a new break-through into a more enlightened state
of consciousness by the meditative practice. Here,
man is learning to utilize his own Light by attuning
it to the Light of Spirit."

Your Wave Length of Light

George Fox's Society of Friends, the Quakers, were originally known as the Children of Light, and this quality has long been associated with the saints, rishis, and gurus. The artists have depicted such a person usually with a halo of light around the head.

It is interesting to know that each individual has his own particular wave-length in relation to the light. Sometimes it is a single color, but invariably the use of several intermingled colors can finally bring that state of unity between man's spirit and a heightened state of awareness.

As is known, light is broken down into the seven spectrum colors, ranging from red, which is the most dense of the lowest vibratory rate, to violet, being the highest color which the human eye can visualize. Of course, many other light vibrations exist beyond the range of the human's capacity to observe.

Your Own Sound Vibration

Each individual also has a sound vibration which commences as one 'quickens' in the embryonic state during pregnancy, at approximately 3½ months. This sound vibration is as individualized as our own fingerprints, our perfume, or our light. However, it can be developed if one wishes to bring about a state of greater attunement with God.

Even as the spectrum colors encompass the normal range of light vibration, there also exists a sound which envelops the whole range of the human vocabulary. This three-lettered word, "AUM," covers every language which has ever been utilized by Man — past, present, and future. Even though it contains only three letters, it occupies the entire vocal cavity of the human mouth.

Sounding the "Aum"

Many readers will recognize the sound, although the meaning is not well-known. If practiced during meditation — either in silence or aloud — it will strengthen the human vibratory wave length.

The word "AUM" normally is pronounced to rhyme with "home." The letter "A" itself, when sounded, commences at the back of the throat and utilizes the local area to the roof of the mouth. The letter "U" begins where the letter A finishes, namely, the back of the mouth to the forward part of our voice mechanism. The final "M" starts from the area just behind the top piece to the closed lips of the speaker.

The practice of this word is, in an auditory sense, one complete and entire system of Yoga which is practiced by some Indian people. However, we incorporate it in our meditation as a means of drawing our consciousness into a more receptive state, so that our inner ears become sensitive to the sound of the Spirit of God.

Awakening Through Meditation

Any person with a normal intelligence can learn deep meditation and can awaken the gifts of the

Spirit. In fact, it is the safest way in which to gain this wonderful privilege which God gives to His Children. The late Arthur Ford once told Rev. Street of how, when he first became acquainted with Paramahansa Yogananda, he was so impressed that he spent the next three years studying meditation with him. We are all aware of the unselfish life of Ford and the evidence which he gave to many people concerning the survival of the human spirit beyond the grave.

Most yogis have the gifts of the Spirit activated in their lives and use them as required. Of course, most of us living a normal work-a-day life cannot spare the time which a yogi spends in meditation and contemplation, yet we can discipline our lives to the extent of utilizing our willpower and learning to meditate. There is no doubt that we are greatly aided in finding the time to grow and develop in this respect. In fact, many times we may be awakened from sleep to meditate. If we remain unselfish in our desire to be of service to our Fellows, rather than wishing to become a magician by practicing some psychic tricks, then more and more help will be extended to us in the spiritual life.

Meditative Technique

To begin meditation, sit quietly in a chair or upright in bed so that the spine is straight. Keep a pencil and notebook by your side, ready to record anything which is "said" to you. Expect Nothing! Conveyances come when they are least expected.

Now with comfortable position assumed and eyes

closed, visualize that you are facing a hillside and are about to ascend to your place of worship, which is some quiet and peaceful spot on this hill.

You are about to walk on the Pathway of Light, and the first step you take is on the color RED. You stand on it and feel the glorious rays of this lovely color all around you. Your whole being becomes suffused with its power.

Quietly and with reverence, step onto the color ORANGE and once again feel its exquisite folds enveloping you.

After savoring the beauty of the heightened vibration, walk on the next step which is YELLOW. It is the color of the sun, and you breathe in its glowing warmth.

Now stand on the color GREEN, which emanates all around you in the verdant shades of the grass and trees.

From here you are approaching the doors of the Temple itself, as you step onto a step of PALE BLUE which wraps you in its splendor and beauty. You pause until your vibration is raised to the rate of this color, then you move on to a DARK BLUE or INDIGO. On this step you again wait, knowing that you are closer to the Holy Portals and need to be further stilled.

At last, you ascend the final step of VIOLET, and standing on the seventh color ray which is the highest vibratory rate discernible to your vision, you are cloaked in regal color.

Suddenly, the doors of the Holy Place are flung open, and you enter in great awe as you have come to meet your Lord. As you kneel before the altar in your sanctuary, visualize that symbol which is most sacred to you, and allow the innermost part of your consciousness to flow in love to your Master.

To most readers a Christian emblem such as a white cross (or a golden cross) will be used, but to others a Buddha or a Star of David which is the highest in a particular religion will be suitable, provided one can identify with it and become offered in adoration to his Lord. Here, the mind has become stabilized by the previous ascent through the colors, and a wonderful symbol will attract your mind and prevent any strain.

Now with the mind at one in a flow of love to your Master, sound the sacred word "AUM," which you will remember rhymes with "home." Practice this chant using the entire range of your voice box. Repeat this sound seven times until you have discovered that a certain composure for quietness has entered your mind and left a state of tranquility.

Long periods of meditation are not recommended, but in this discipline we resemble flowers which benefit from daily attention. So the seeker after new truth will want to practice this first form of early meditation wherein he reaches the altar and begins to experience the beauty and depth of the Silence itself for some ten to fifteen minutes a day. This practice is best carried out at the same time and in the same place.

To return to normal consciousness is just as important as entering into the higher realms of Spirit. After remaining in the Silence, we break off the tie to return to the body via the mind. This is best accomplished by reversing the process of ascent by a descent through the spectrum-colored stairs, i.e., Violet, Dark and Pale Blues, Green, Yellow, Orange, and Red, to the earth below.

If one is able to study this technique with a group of persons (three people are better than two), the power developed is greatly enhanced by a collective meditation, as the group commences to develop a soul of its own.

The best time for personal development is early in the morning. If it is put off until late at night, the individual is usually too tired to benefit from it, and that is one of the reasons so many people say that they cannot meditate.

Travel Slowly on the Path

The practice of deep meditation is recommended as a gradual development. We are all eternal beings with all the time we need before us. It is far better to travel slowly and securely than to try to speed up our evolutionary progress by excessive zeal, which frequently is a cause of disturbance in our lives. Rev. Street's own personal development is a marvelous example of waiting with patience, and the great value of his life in service to others quite aptly speaks for itself.

A Change In Dreams

Very quickly after beginning meditation, one will find that his dreams have altered. This change can be directly attributed to an enlightenment of consciousness that has cleared away some of the debris in the mind. Heretofore, there has been an obstruction to learning at night. Now the doors are open for instruction of a psychic nature to be conveyed during sleep.

Frequently, persons will begin to see faces before them as they retire, or during meditation they may see an eye, which is a very clear indication that Spirit is watching — a wonderful sign of a universal nature.

It is important to keep a pencil and notebook by the bed during sleep, because conveyances will be offered which, if recorded, will form a tangible link with Spirit. Invariably, a portion of the dream or vision will re-enter the mind during the day when one is not thinking of it.

As one progresses, his dreams in color will be an excellent indication that he is being tutored by Spirit teachers, as color dreams usually denote spirit conveyances rather than dreams formed from the subconscious mind.

In a later chapter, a more identifiable technique is shown which can take the aspirant to a heightened state of receptivity. But NOTE, PLEASE!: Never attempt advanced meditation until you have gained a firm footing in the Silence by the preliminary method unfolded in this chapter. Otherwise, you will cast away an oar which will help keep your boat guided and afloat. This premature haste will only slow spiritual progress in the long run.

A Clinical Approach to Meditation

Many clinical studies have been carried out to determine the physiological changes which occur during meditation. Basic considerations in such a study usually include the measurement of oxygen consumption and metabolic rate, along with determining alpha-wave activity through an electroencephalograph (EEG). Various results of the findings differ from researcher to researcher due to a variety of subjects, testing conditions, etc.

However, the general consensus points to the idea that meditation induces a state which is completely different from normal consciousness (i.e., wakefulness, sleeping, or dreaming). Carried a little further, in a case of altered consciousness such as hypnosis, the meditative state is still in its own category due to the discovery that most hypnotic patterns seem to resemble the waking state.

Drugs and Meditation

For anyone who has practiced meditation for any length of time, it is obvious that the continued discipline does invoke experiences of a psychic nature. For instance, it is not uncommon for a person to see a kaleidoscope of varied colors and patterns which swirl and alter at a rhythmed pace.

At the same time, a person who has taken a certain drug may have known a similar experience. So the question arises: "Why not take drugs to create this state?"

Granted, a certain level of visual stimulation will probably occur with the use of drugs. However, it must be added that the drug state is, in a sense, an artificial fantasy. Spiritual attunement is a state which is arrived at through discipline, not an intake of chemical agents into the body. On one hand, true meditation is a state of spiritual *being,* while drug stimulation is an incomplete bridge into spiritual experience.

Using the Meditative State

In discussing the advantages of a meditative state, most clinicians will agree that meditation can have practical therapeutic value when it comes to relieving physical and mental tension.

An example of applying this method of relaxation came from a man who had been taught a little about meditation from a group of friends in California. After practicing the discipline for a very short period, the man had to go to the hospital unexpectedly for a series of laboratory tests. One of the tests labored on for seven hours and was quite painful. By the third hour, the patient was greatly vexed from the effects of the strain, when suddenly he remembered that he could, in a sense, ''deaden'' the experience by inducing the meditative state. Immediately, he went into the Silence, attuning his consciousness to a higher state.

Telling of the experience later, he was amazed at the change which had overcome him, for most of the mental tension had dissipated along with the dread of the physical pain. Three years later, the practice of meditation has become an indispensable part of his growth and development.

A sketch of Noel Street's humor, which is never nestled far from the surface, is portrayed in an experience he had not long ago. He was in a public build-

ing and had just stepped onto an elevator. As the
doors clamped shut and the box moved upward, the
whole mechanism jammed, leaving a band of hysterical people suspended between two floors. Amidst a
reign of confusion and varied comments, Rev. Street
calmly sat down on the floor and began to meditate.
His explanation seemed reasonable enough: ''Well,
I knew that words and emotion would do little to get.
me out — what's more, I was helping to reduce the
oxygen consumption!''

As one begins daily communion with God, a
strong bond is formed, which is spoken of so beautifully in the words of an Eskimo:

> ''The great sea moves me,
> The vault of heaven moves me,
> And I tremble with joy!''

Chapter 8

The Miracle of YOU!

The Psychic Centers in the Body

Even as meditation can alter the "light" composition of our physical body, so too does this practice help to awaken the psychic energies or forces within and surrounding our physical body.

The seat of the soul is named by the Ancients as the pineal gland, which is situated roughly in the center of the head. When awakened, it becomes what is commonly called our Third Eye, and provides "second sight" or clairvoyance. Such an awakened state of this particular gland causes the soul to enter into illumination and the light (depicted around the heads of spiritually-minded persons) commences to develop. Merely by placing the hands on the top of the head of an individual who has led a spiritual life, one can readily feel a glow just above the fonteneal, indicating the attunement with Spirit.

As the student commences to meditate, this state of enlightenment proceeds throughout the body via the connecting glands which relate to the pineal.

The second gland contacted is the pituitary gland, which is just in front of the pineal and is called the "father of the endocrine glandular orchestra." It is the first active gland related to the over-all growth of our physical bodies.

From there the power descends to the thyroid gland in the throat, referred to as the "mother of the endocrine orchestra," Downwards the flow continues to the heart area or love center from which come the terms "brokenhearted," "softhearted," and so on.

Next, the flow reaches the "mechanical brain" or solar plexus. Actually, this portion is the area where part of the subconscious mind is housed, and quite mysteriously, it is connected with our spirit consciousness or memory of past lives.

Continuing the pathway of the incoming light flow, we find the next center in the spine to be opposite the navel, and it is especially important when awakened as the physical consciousness begins to move upwards into more spiritual atmospheres.

Lastly, the light descends to the chakra at the base of the spine which is really a storehouse of the Kundalini sex force. The chakra serves also as a relay station for the energy forces which come from the center of the earth and pass through the base of the spine. It is interesting to note that this is the power used by persons practicing radiaesthesia, generally.

As the Kundalini power awakens in the aspirant, the force commences to rise up the spinal cord, until it is finally transmuted. However, this topic will be dealt with in greater detail in Chapter 13, "Kundalini and Sex."

"On the Path"

After we commence meditating, our bodies become influenced by the incoming divine force and tend to become "lighter" in texture. This occurrence is obvious, because the normal state is a purely commercial frame of mind wherein the main concern is with the physical or everyday matters and not spiritual interests. And as soon as the spiritual side of our nature starts to awaken, then the physical side gives up some of its potency. As our bodies become less dense and illumination begins, we are truly "on the path" to enlightenment.

Correct eating habits also influence the density of the body, and often the aspirant finds that he is no longer interested in eating foods which have a strong taste. Quite frequently, too, the individual will desire to eliminate certain practices in his life that may be injurious to his health — such as taking alcohol, smoking, and possibly eating meat in excess. And not only do we feel much better because of these removals, but our body is cleaner in every way.

The Etheric Body

The etheric body is a duplicate of the physical body and usually extends slightly outside it, interpenetrating to some extent. Being greatly influenced by our habits, the etheric body is easily poisoned if an individual is a heavy smoker, due to the way the smoke is "locked" in and cannot escape from the atmosphere. Consequently, the smoker is constantly breathing polluted air.

The Astral Body

The astral body is separate from the etheric; it is the body of our spiritual nature which stays with us after the physical body has gone back into the earth, taking with it the etheric mold.

Pressures and Illness

As soon as pressure is placed on one of the bodies, for whatever reason, a cutting off of the life force in that body is inevitable. And if this blockage proceeds to form an illness in the dense physical body, which is usually the case, then the healer is required not only to treat the physical body but the other bodies as well — namely, the emotional, mental and spiritual vehicles. The etheric body is a shadow of the physical form, but if differs from the others in that it has no will of its own.

The illness always develops in the weakest area or areas. In the healer's effort to restore the life force, he must be conscious of what he is attempting to do. The treatment involves much more than placing a hand on a person's body and hoping that an organ will be restored to normal working order in some miraculous way. Because the illness has required a good deal of pressure to develop, considerable effort will need to be exerted to remove it.

Eventually, the healer will notice certain signs about his patient, one of which is the fact that the life force in the person can be greatly influenced when the healing power is received without difficulty. This easy receptivity of power into the body is fairly unusual nowadays, because so many persons are taking vitamins or drugs promiscuously.

Quite often Rev. Street finds this information on vitamin therapy to be poorly received by persons who react by saying, "The vitamins I take are all organically grown," or alternatively, "I only take the purest of vitamins into my body, and they are very helpful to my health." From his experience, however, he feels that very few people are taking vitamins beneficially.

"There may be a good initial reaction, but after a little while this wears off, and generally, people take far too many vitamins with the result that their body reacts in a sluggish way," he says.

Unfortunately, today nearly all drugs act on the whole of the body. Thus, a person taking a pain-killer for his arthritis will simultaneously develop other difficulties, because all the organs of the body become deadened and less than normally effective due to the semi-drugged condition.

The nervous system, if drugged, is far less capable of receiving the healing force. Thus, to be free of drugs or vitamins in the system prior to the healing treatment is highly recommended.

Applying the Healing Force Correctly

The right side of the body is positive, while the left side is negative. And it is beneficial for the healer to be able to apply correctly the right force to the

right part of the body of his patient. (This practice
is carefully explained in the chapter on Noel Street's
healing techniques.)

So even as the life force makes contact with the
pineal gland initially, it then continues to flow down
the spinal cord through the motor and sensory
nerves, continuing to flow to all the terminals of
the body. As a result, every part of the body is in
closer touch with the Divine life essence, which ultimately is sustained by right diet, thought, and
spirit.

ORGANS OF THE HUMAN BODY

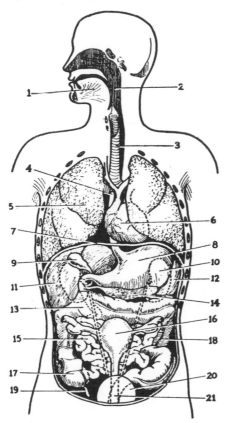

1. Tongue	8. Stomach	15. Small intestines
2. Pharynx or throat	9. Gall bladder	16. Uterus
3. Trachea or windpipe	10. Kidney	17. Cecum
4. Esophagus	11. Liver	18. Descending colon
5. Lung	12. Spleen	19. Appendix
6. Heart	13. Colon	20. Bladder—urinary
7. Diaphragm	14. Pancreas	21. Sigmoid

GLANDULAR CENTERS USED IN PSYCHIC HEALING

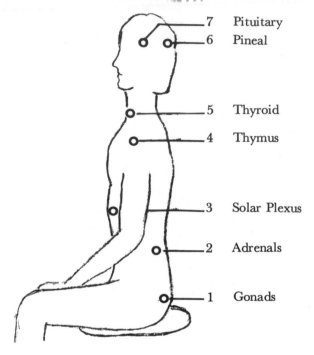

7   Pituitary
6   Pineal

5   Thyroid
4   Thymus

3   Solar Plexus

2   Adrenals

1   Gonads

(1)	MULADHARA	CHAKRA
(2)	SVADHISTHANA	,,
(3)	MANIPURA	,,
(4)	ANAHATA	,,
(5)	VISHUDORA	,,
(6)	AJNA	,,
(7)	SAHASRARA	,,

These Glandular Centers (Chakras) play a vital part in the healing techniques shown in diagrams 1-11 pages 136-141.

Chapter 9

Eating Pure Food

The United States today is showing an uncommon interest in the revival of pure food eating, and this movement is under tremendous pressure created by the vested interest groups of retail manufacturers who sell through the supermarket chains.

Throughout the country many "new thought" people are identifying with the production of pure foods as well as the sale of it. Of course, this awakening correlates with the interests in all forms of natural life now occuring in America. It seems inevitable that food manufacturers will ultimately be concerned with giving the customer the best product, in terms of tastier food, as well as making available that food which is more beneficial to the body's good health.

U.S.D.A. Report

With a growing interest in staying healthy through better nutrition, a shopper may be quite confused by all the talk on "health" foods. Does a higher nutritional value really exist in certain types of foods, and if so, is the hiked price in health food stores justified?

This question involves conflicting answers from food chemists and nutritionists. Some experts claim that eating organically grown foods is the only guarantee one has from slowly poisoning himself. The other extreme suggests that the neighborhood super-market is fully able to provide a family with all the safe, nutritious food it needs.

Whatever the final outcome of this particular query, most people will usually agree that super-markets are less expensive, but health foods are more palatable.

Below is a chart encasing a breakdown in certain nutrients contained in bread, rice, and sugar.

BREAD — 100 gram portion

	Protein	Calcium	Phosphorus	Potassium
Whole-grain	10.5 g.	99 mg.	228 mg.	273 mg.
Enriched white	8.7 g.	85 mg.	97 mg.	105 mg.

Iron and various B vitamins are fairly equal.

RICE

"Instant" rice is lower in nutrients, while "con-verted" rice retains most of its nutrients.

	Calcium	Potassium
Instant	23 mg.	None
Converted	272 mg.	680 mg.
Brown	145 mg.	971 mg.

SUGAR

	Calcium	Potassium
White	None	14 mg.
Brown	386 mg.	1560 mg.

Brown sugar is also abundant in iron and phosphorus, comparatively.

Vegetarian Diet

It was with some doubt that I first began to consider the pros and cons of a vegetarian diet. For one thing, I had a preconceived notion that a person could not maintain good health without eating meat, and this conditioned thinking seemed to minimize the belief that the protein content in non-meat products is sufficient.

However, in hearing Rev. Street lecture on vegetarian diet, I decided that I would like to give it a try. My main motivation was due to the fact that I did not particularly like the taste of meat, and it always left me feeling sluggish and heavy.

So, doing a little research on the content of certain vitamin and protein values in various foods, I experimented with a vegetarian diet for six weeks. In making the transition, I ate fish occasionally in the place of meat and included liberal portions of milk, eggs, cheese, nuts, and beans, along with an increase in fresh fruits and vegetables.

You may be wondering how I got along with the change. Well, the diet was so much more satisfying to me than I ever expected and left me with much more energy, so that what started out to be a six-week experiment ended as a permanent diet!

After several months of vegetarian cookery, I began to eat even more fresh fruits and vegetables, as I have found the raw form to be excellent. In any form of processing, food value is destroyed to some extent, so the more the intake of raw foods, the richer will be the source of nutrients gained.

Meat eaters may be interested to know that meat

when swallowed, requires twenty-four hours to pass through the body of a person with an average digestive system. In comparison, fish (which is the next highest source of protein) requires only five hours to be eliminated from the body. The main advantage in relation to this observation is in the lesser strain that is placed on the heart during digestion. Furthermore, the decomposition of meat in the body releases toxic gases in the system.

The Mercury Scare

Today there is a great deal of discussion on the mercury content in fish, and some meat eaters are noticeably pleased with this development. It is interesting to point out, however, that the human body is quick to develop a resistance to any substance which may be poisonous to some extent. This adaptation is one of the most remarkable features of human life — namely, our ability to adjust to the environment.

Obviously, if a person smokes, takes alcohol, consumes drugs, or takes large amounts of coffee, the taste buds will be somewhat impaired so that this change in diet will seem too mild to them. Especially would the switch to raw fruits and vegetables seem bland. But as we seek a healthier body through right eating, we will come to appreciate the taste of an apple or an orange which still has some of the life force in it.

"Mental" Vegetarians

It must be stressed here that some persons are "mental" vegetarians, as their bodies simply cannot assimilate sufficient protein from sources of food other than meat. In this matter of nutrition, we all remain individuals and must find the diet which best suits each one of us.

In my own case, I have never sought to be a reformer in this matter. At one time I smoked two packages of cigarettes a day. But, like meat-eating, I eliminated this practice from my life in seeking to live closer to the Spirit through good health. And should anyone be interested in knowing why I have changed, or how, I am always happy to share my experience with him.

A diet that is perfect for you may not necessarily be right for another member of your family. But most people like to experiment in their kitchens with various vegetarian recipes in learning to cook without meat. Should anyone be interested in reading an excellent book written by Noel Street's wife, Colleen, (who is the co-director of the Lotus Ashram in Miami) may I recommend *Colleen's Cookbook*. In this book are practical tips in making dietary changes from meat-eating to vegetarianism, which are both palatable and economical.

One can never over-emphasize the fact that the aspirant on the spiritual path should never get too caught up in anything which draws attention to himself. And this warning applies to diet as well as any development and growth in a spiritual sense. Initially, when we first come across anything which is evolutionary in our lives, we are inclined to speak of it too openly — often boring friends and family. Therefore, it is wise to be reticent in speaking of our activities.

Quite often, we see humorous examples of "die-hards" who would contradict *any* approach. On one occasion a very zealous young health lecturer referred to honey as a food which no normal-minded person would take, as it is the "vomit of bees!"

So with this notion in mind, we can readily believe that no matter what we believe, someone who is doing the very opposite will decry our values. Hence, it is prudent to keep a still tongue, and proceed quietly as one feels impressed to do. And if one is in any doubt about a certain problem, he may ask for guidance while in the Silence, knowing that help will come in one form or another.

Natural Sources of Vitamins

A section has been included here for anyone who is interested in familiarizing himself with various vitamin contents in foods. It is an excellent guide when seeking to plan a proper diet containing the necessary nutrients for good health.

VITAMIN A

Characteristics: fat soluble, destroyed by high temperatures when oxygen is present.

Builds new body cells, promotes growth, helps body resist infection, essential for normal tooth formation, healthy skin and mucus membranes. Prevents the development of nutritional night blindness. Aids in normal pregnancy and lactation.

A deficiency of this vitamin in the diet results in retarded growth, reduced resistance to infections,

respiratory infections, rough, dry skin, night blindness, conjunctiva, trachea, degeneration of spinal
cord and interference with reproduction.

Sources are alfalfa sprouts, cheese, milk, butter,
cream, eggs, yellow corn, winter squash, carrots,
sweet potatoes, tomatoes, peas, green beans, escarole,
kale, parsley, prunes, pineapples, oranges, limes,
cantaloupes, peaches, avocados, apricots.

VITAMIN B COMPLEX

This is a combination of a large number of water-
soluble vitamins, isolated from liver, yeast, and
other sources.

Characteristics: may be destroyed by excessive
heating of 2-4 hours. Soda in cooking aids in destruction.

Among vitamins included in this group are
thiamine (B_1), riboflavin (B_2), niacin, pyridoxin
(B_6), biotin, inositol, p-aminobenzoic acid (PABA),
cyanocobalamine (B_{12}), and folic acid.

Affects normal growth, healthy skin and eyes,
normal pregnancy and lactation, gastrointestinal,
nervous and endocrine systems, appetite. Reduces
sugar content in diabetes, aids in tuberculosis, stimu-
lates biliary action and is necessary for carbohydrate
metabolism.

A deficiency leads to beriberi, pellagra, digestive
disturbances, enlargement of the liver, reduction of
pancreas, affects the thyroid, causes degeneration of
sex glands, reduces catalysis of tissues, skin lesions
about the face and mouth, possible nervous afflictions,
deranges the endocrines, induces edema, affects the

heart, liver, spleen and kidneys, and may cause
enlargement of the adrenals.

It is found in whole grains, fish, eggs, legumes,
nuts, bran, rice, green leafy vegetables, tomatoes,
fruits, peas, soybean milk, alfafa and soy bean
sprouts, cheese, brewer's yeast, wheat germ.

VITAMIN B₁

(Thiamine hydrochloride, antineuritic vitamin)
One fraction of Vitamin B complex.

Characteristics: destroyed by long exposure to
heat and oxidation. Soda in cooking water aids
in destruction. Water soluble.

This vitamin is essential for normal growth,
normal functioning of the digestive system and
maintenance of appetite, healthy nerves, normal
pregnancy and lactation. Essential also for proper
utilization of sugars and starches, normal tone
and functioning of the digestive tract.

A lack of this vitamin in the diet may result in
loss of appetite, impaired digestion of starches and
sugars, colitis, constipation or diarrhea, emaciation,
loss of muscular coordination, beriberi, nervous
disorders of various types.

Foods rich in Vitamin B₁ are whole grain cereals,
alfafa sprouts, soybean milk, legumes, nuts, peas,
green leafy vegetables, bananas, apples, avocados,
citrus fruits, milk, brewer's yeast, wheat germ.

VITAMIN B₂

(Riboflavin or Vitamin G) A component of
Vitamin B complex.

Characteristics: water soluble, alcohol soluble, heat stable, unstable to light.

Required for normal growth and development, healthy skin and eyes. Its primary bodily function deals with the oxidation within the cells.

A deficiency in the diet may cause impaired growth, fatigue, weakness, headaches, skin lesions about the mouth and face, and pale lips.

Valuable sources are alfafa and soybean sprouts, green leafy vegetables, milk, cheese, eggs, tomatoes, oranges, bananas, citrus fruits, apricots, legumes, seeds, peas, whole grains, brewer's yeast, wheat germ.

NIACIN

(Nicotinic Acid, nicotinamide antipellegra vitamin)

Characteristics: water soluble, not destroyed by heat, light, air, or alkali.

Necessary for normal development and growth, normal functioning of gastro-intestinal tract, healthy clear skin.

Deficiency results are mental disturbances, gastro-intestinal disturbances, pellagra, blacktongue (in dogs).

Natural sources of this vitamin are legumes, milk, green leafy vegetables, tomatoes, whole grains, alfafa sprouts, natural rice, peanuts, mushrooms, brewer's yeast, wheat germ.

BIOTIN

(Formerly known as Vitamin H) A part of Vitamin B complex.

Though the effects of biotin deficiency have been determined in animals, such effects in man remain unconfirmed

INOSITOL

(Hexahydroxycyclohexane, a sugarlike crystalline substance) Also a fraction of Vitamin B complex, · found in the liver, kidneys, skeletal and heart muscles. Also present in the leaves and seeds of most plants and vegetables.

Although still in the experimental stages, a deficiency results in loss of hair, eye defects and retardation of growth.

VITAMIN B_{12}

(Cyanocobalamine,   anti-pernicious   anemia principle) A complex discovery, dating from 1948.

It is used in minute doses for treatment of pernicious anemia, spinal collapse. Essential for formation of red blood cells. It is helpful for some skin complaints, intestinal disorders, diarrhea, ulcerated lips, sore mouths and throats, nervous complaints.

A deficiency may be the result of a diet with too little protein.

This vitamin can be extracted from soy beans, natural rice, bran, legumes, nuts, milk, eggs, brewer's yeast.

FOLIC ACID

(Pteroylglutamic acid; once known as Vitamin M) Component of Vitamin B complex.

Used in treating pernicious anemia, macrocytic

anemia, celiac syndrome, sprue, menstrual problems, and is essential for a normal, healthy pregnancy.

Lack of it causes over-large red blood cells that act abnormally.

Found in green leaves, navy beans, asparagus, nuts, brewer's yeast.

VITAMIN C

(Ascorbic Acid)

Characteristics: lost in cooking unless container is airtight, soluble in water, lost in storage if exposed to air, nutritional value greatly lost in canning and freezing of foods.

Essential for normal growth and development and the formation of intercellular substance of connective tissue (collagen). Also for the maintenance of practically all body tissue, especially those having to do with joint structures, bones, teeth, gums, and ligaments. Remedial for hemorrhages, brittle bones and tuberculosis, pneumonia, diptheria, whooping cough, rheumatic fever, rheumatoid arthritis, hay fever, burns, as well as increasing bodily resistance to infection.

A deficiency leads to tender joints, lowered resistance to infections, tooth decay, pyorrhea, and bleeding gums, anemia, injury to bone cells and blood vessels, scurvy.

Vitamin C foods are fruits and vegetables such as strawberries, apples, pears, apricots, plums, peaches, pineapples, lemons, grapefruit, cantaloupes, mangoes, guava, oranges, raw cabbage, carrots, potatoes, lettuce, celery, onions, tomatoes, radishes, green peppers.

VITAMIN D

(Calciferol) The Sunlight Vitamin!

Characteristics. stored in liver in the body, relatively stable under refrigeration.

Regulates the utilization of calcium and phosphorus in the development of bones and teeth, normalizes blood, essential for normal growth and development, healthy nerves and resistance to infection, as well as correct circulation. It is especially beneficial for infants, and women during pregnancy and lactation.

A deficiency results in imperfect skeletal formation, tooth decay, nervous disorders, irritability, lowered resistance to infection, rickets in children and osteomalacia in adults.

Natural sources of this vitamin are butter, egg yolk, cream, milk, sunflower seeds, almonds, coconut, brewer's yeast and, of course, SUNLIGHT! (The exposure to the sun or ultra-violet ray synthesizes Vitamin D in the body.)

VITAMIN E

(Alpha tocopherol) Staff of Life Vitamin!

Characteristics: fat soluble, stable to heat.

Associated with reproduction function. May prevent difficult birth and muscular dystrophy. Aids lactation in mothers, has proved beneficial in treatment of burns when applied directly to the skin, and also most helpful in heart conditions.

A deficiency may result in lack of fertility or reproductive powers, late maturity and infrequent ovulation.

Vitamin E is available in celery, lettuce, beets, green leafy vegetables, seeds, nuts, oranges, olive oil, flax oil, cottonseed oil, wheat germ.

VITAMIN K

(Blood coagulation vitamin)

Aids in blood coagulation and is necessary for formation of prothrombin. It is needed for good circulation and is anti-hemorrhagic. The vitamin is used to eliminate prolonged bleeding in operations and in biliary tract of jaundiced patients.

Natural sources are alfalfa sprouts, oats, wheat, rye, and green leafy vegetables.

VITAMIN P

(Citrin) Associated with Vitamin C.

Prevents black and blue marks following blows, helps to prevent bleeding and scurvy and is essential for normal integrity of capillary membranes and normal permeability.

Deficiency results in easy bruising and bleeding.

Sources are lime juice, lemons, grapefruits, oranges, and red peppers.

Chapter 10

Health Tips for Better Living

In his years as a healer, Rev. Street has found certain health tips to be applicable to most patients. The suggestions included here are some of those tips — both on a dietary and personal level.*

Using a Vegetable Steamer

A valuable hint in the preparation of food lies in the scrubbing rather than peeling of vegetables, as much of the nutritional value lies just under the skin and is lost when peeled away.

To complement taste, the steaming method seems to be the superior method of cooking for several reasons. For one thing, the mineral and vitamin content is preserved. Too often, nutritional benefit of the food is lost before it is ever served, as the juice is poured down the sink!

Another advantage of the steamer is the convenience allowed in cooking all vegetables together, if desired. As the steam comes in contact with the vegetables, the pores close on the different foods, and thus, the tastes are not intermingled.

---

* All products specifically mentioned in this chapter are directly available from The Lotus Ashram, 128 NE 82nd Terrace, Miami, Florida 33138.

Because many people have written to Mrs. Street concerning the availability of vegetable steamers, she has worked to develop an excellent, low-cost steamer with a stainless steel base which is available at the Lotus Ashram.

A Recommended Beverage

Quite often, a person may wish to eliminate caffeine from the diet in an effort to improve health, and many coffee and tea substitutes are available at health food stores.

While on the last national lecture tour, Rev. Street had the privilege of visiting the Hilltop Herb Farm in Cleveland, Texas. It was there that he met the owner, Mrs. Madeline Hill, who has created a lovely blend of tea containing eighteen herbs. Called "tranquili-tea," the mixture is especially beneficial when taken before bedtime, as it acts to calm the nerves. The herbs have not been sprayed with any chemicals, and Rev. Street found the taste so delightful, that he now stocks it at the Miami Center at 85¢ a package.

Salt

When steaming vegetables, it is unlikely that the addition of any extra salt will be necessary as the vegetable has retained its natural salts during preparation.

When buying vegetable salt, it is recommended that a brand be purchased which does not contain more than a limited per centage of sodium chloride. In order to save money on production costs, some manufacturers have been known to add nearly half sodium chloride to the package. However, a law now requires better standards insuring an improved product.

Eggs

Today the supermarkets carry a wide range of eggs varying in size, and sometimes color. However, the fact that most of the eggs have been obtained from battery-kept fowl, undoubtedly leaves the egg with an inferior taste. Occasionally, yard eggs are available, but in areas adjacent to cities, the battery-fed poultry eggs are usually the only kind which can be found.

To those persons who love animals, it is quite sad that such conditions as the battery farms exist for the sole purpose of profit.

Rev. Street once told me of an experience which he had while standing outside such a farm where the chickens were treated so cruelly. He was able to hear clairaudiently the cry of the poor imprisoned creatures — a sound of extreme anguish rising upward over the area where the chickens were housed.

It is hoped that law will soon prevent owners from enforcing such vicious conditions on the lesser creatures, for under the present system the chickens can not lead any semblance of a normal life — they cannot run about or fly, they cannot take a dust bath, experience motherhood, or just enjoy being in the flock with the others. Instead, they must spend their lives in a cage, never walking, only producing for the sake of monetary gain — a deplorable form of exploitation!

Under such unnatural living conditions, it is no wonder that the eggs are so poor in taste. With the growing interest in ecology, perhaps these prison farms will be short-lived, ultimately, making better eggs available.

Salads

Many delicious salads can be easily prepared for entire meals, if a person desires to have food with an abundance of life force in it. Such vegetables which make an excellent mixture are lettuce, water cress, cucumber, tomato, radish, escarole, spring onions, and beet root.

Other more unusual ingredients include mustard greens, nasturtium leaves, dandelions, endive, and chicory. All these items combine to make a delicious and refreshing salad to which can be added chopped parsley and other delightful herbs. Served with a potato (in the skin), cheese, or eggs, these meals are quick and easy to prepare.

Sprouting Seeds

Another good source of food with abundant life force is easily sprouted right in your own kitchen. Adding variety in texture and color to the diet, sprouted seeds are rich in vitamins and minerals. They are excellent when sprinkled on salads, soups, sandwiches, and baked dishes.

In experimenting, Mrs. Street has found the following seeds to be very good for sprouting: alfalfa seeds, fava beans, sprouting wheat, mung beans, chick peas, lentils, and sprouting soy beans.

Through her own interest in good health, she has developed a "Home Sprouting Lid-Kit," which is also available at $1.50 and $1.75 per kit. The set is complete with full instructions for home use.

Over the past fifteen years, Rev. Street has found the following suggestions to be of immense value in patient healing.

1. SHOES

The avoidance of wearing shoes with rubber soles is highly recommended, as this and other in-sulating materials tend to block out the life force coming from the earth and entering our body through the soles of the feet. Likewise, the stale ethers being released from the feet are blocked in by rubber. Some better materials to have next to the foot are leather, rope or cork.

Another practice which allows the feet to "breathe" and receive life force was conveyed to Rev. Street from Spirit. It involves walking barefoot in the dewy grass early in the morning and letting the moisture completely soak the skin.

As a healer, these suggestions are especially im-portant, as they tend to make a great difference in developing the healing power within the body.

2. SLEEP

For those persons who have difficulty in sleeping, several suggestions may be made here.

First, avoid any stimulants such as regular coffee or tea before retiring; warm milk with honey is an excellent drink before bedtime which usually induces a relaxed state for sleep.

A certain method which Rev. Street uses is carried out specifically to relax a tense body. Lying on the back, visualize your head becoming very heavy and sinking through the pillows. Next, the neck receives this heaviness, and it further spreads to the shoulders, one arm, the other arm, the chest, stomach, pelvis, one leg, the other leg, one foot, and finally the other foot. With passive mind, the whole body has become heavy and very relaxed. If necessary, repeat the process — always quite slowly — this time commencing from the feet upward.

Now, with the body and muscles as relaxed as possible, sound the affirmation "UNITROL." This word is one which contains in its sound all the vibrations of sound sleep in the universe and has proven to be extremely effective in quieting the mind and body. It should be repeated slowly and aloud, three times, to be most effective.

A final suggestion for achieving sound sleep is usually found in placing the bed in the direction of East and West. Such an arrangement has a remarkable effect. Often said to be related to magnet flow and earth polarities, most sleepers will find this change to be a real improvement over the North-South position.

3. IODINE

Many people have a deficiency in iodine within their bodies, resulting in an undernourished thyroid gland. An excellent way to abate this deficiency is to paint a strip (using iodine tincture) just below the navel, making it about a foot long and an inch wide; do this before going to bed at night. If the person is actually deficient, he will find the next morning that the dark brown color has lost its potency and is a pale yellow or completely gone.

A nightly application is recommended, until the strip remains the same color the next morning as it was when first applied. With this result achieved, the body has temporarily "taken in" enough iodine for the time being, and does not need any more for several days or a week. The individual can easily gauge this need by applying iodine at intervals and checking the amount that goes into the body.

This method is especially helpful for those persons who are allergic to iodine in tablet form. Furthermore, it provides a way of achieving a balance without forcing a set amount of drug into the body unnecessarily and is a much more natural method of treatment.

4. EYES

Some years ago, a physician in New York named Dr. Benjamin wrote a book called *Better Sight Without Glasses*. The method he prescribed for improving vision has proved to be helpful to thousands of persons when practiced regularly. The instructions are as follows:

Each day stand before a window, placing one hand over one eye, leaving the other eye open to move from the immediate area to the farthest spot that can be viewed in the distance.

Now, close the eye and open the other one, bringing the point of focus from the horizon back to the area directly before you.

Repeat this cycle continuing for five times, or practice it several times a day, Designed for persons of all ages, it can be beneficial in improving vision and strengthening eye muscles.

5. ARTHRITIS

This condition is usually caused by over-acidity in the body, created either through diet or worry. The first recommendation is to increase the intake of alkaline foods to re-establish the right currents for the reception of the life force into the body.

At the same time, some help can be derived by cutting a potato in half and taking two slices from the center; cut no thicker than a potato chip, apply one piece to the arch area of each foot. The benefit is usually seen within 24 hours, as acid is drawn out of the body through the feet and into the potato slices. The amount of acid can be readily detected through the color which the potato has incurred, as the acid will turn it dark. The amount of acid drawn out decreases with time.

The potato, of course, must be changed daily.

6. KIDNEYS

The use of parsley has proved to be an excellent aid for persons suffering with kidney problems. This herb is rich in mineral salts and is also effective in producing an alkaline state within the body. Whether eaten raw or added to a cooked dish, several sprigs should be consumed daily.

7. LIVER

Leaf sage is most helpful in treating heartburn

or indigestion. Boil a teaspoon of the herb and leave it soaking overnight; drinking it first thing in the morning, this remedy will produce a most effective result in the body. Repeat, if necessary.

8. BREATHING FOR CONFIDENCE

For those persons wishing to induce a state of self-confidence, prior to an interview or before delivering a speech, perhaps, the reinforcement of pranic content in the body is easily attained.

Sitting quietly, take a deep breath and hold the lungs full of air for a slow count of five. Then exhale and leave the lungs empty for the slow count of five. (Usually this time is equivalent to five heartbeats.) Repeat this pattern five times, and an immediate effect will be felt.

This practice is sometimes known as "charging the body with prana," and it is simply an excessive intake of life force from the atmosphere.

One must be careful not to do this late in the evening, as overstimulation will cause difficulty in sleeping. Also, refrain from practicing it more than two or three times daily.

Chapter 11

Noel Street's Own Healing Techniques

Comparative Healing Techniques

The positions listed here are those which Noel Street has found most practical in his healing ministry and are the result of many years' experimentation in various forms of psychic healing. They are direct, precise, and very effective. And any aspiring healer, provided he has learned to tune in to Spirit in meditation, will find great benefit in using them.

It is interesting to notice the various ways in which prominent healers make use of Spirit power. For example, the work of England's Harry Edwards is no more or less effective than the healing ministry of Katherine Kuhlman in the United States. By contrast, we could include the modus operandi of the Philippine "psychic surgeons."

The method is not so important as the result which comes, because the healer is only there to produce an alleviation of the sickness. Therefore, he becomes attuned in spirit to act as a channel for the therapeutic force, and no one other than the patient can claim that any one method is more effective than another.

Mr. Harry Edwards affirms that his power comes from the spirits of "dead doctors," whereas his associates in his healing sanctuary in England indicate that the Holy Spirit is the source of their healing power. Kathryn Kuhlman, on the other hand, in vokes the name of Jesus and prays that she may be removed from her body, as this Spirit occupies it for the period of her healing demonstrations. Thousands of people have witnessed her work which has brought relief to countless numbers of sick people.

The psychic surgery of the Philippines is performed, apparently, by the ability to penetrate the physical body without instruments and perform surgical operations.

Psychometry and Healing

The practice of *psychometry* is a useful aid for the development of clairvoyance. This can be done by anyone who practices meditation. It is true to say that most healers have studied psychometry at the outset of their careers. A good way to practice this is in a small group, placing unidentified articles in an envelope. The leader will have a list of what is inside each envelope. Envelopes can be numbered (example: 1-10). Passing around the group, one writes down the impressions he receives on the contents of each envelope when it comes to him. Some truly fascinating and remarkably evidential results can come from this practice.

Mind and Spirit

No one could ever be able to state authoritatively where mind ends and spirit begins, and it is regrettable that some persons are not able to discern the capacities of Spirit power. Perhaps in time when clairvoyant diagnosis and clairvoyance itself become more recognized, we will find a more complete answer to this fascinating question.

Noel Street's Techniques

In truth, the matter of healing techniques is an individual choice. Rev. Street prefers the ancient techniques illustrated herein. It is a method of power-transmission from healer to patient which is extremely efficient and health-producing. Not only has it been used for many thousands of years in many different parts of the world, but it is very natural and permits a healer to deal with many cases one after the other without becoming excessively tired.

In the healing techniques below, the reader will find that the drawings correspond with the description to aid him in correct application of techniques.

Diagnosing Illness Through Nerve-endings in the Feet

(See charts pp. 128-9)

Until the Healer has gained sufficient experience in being able to diagnose accurately by psychic means, an excellent method of confirming "impressions" of what may be causing the illness is through touching the endings of the nerves in the patient's feet.

The nerve system of the human body ends in specific locations in both hands and feet. It is more difficult to locate the terminals in the hands, as the feet are generally much more sensitive as they are

1   Headaches

2   Pineal Gland

3   Heart

4   Lungs

5   Spine Throat

6   Spine Heart

7   Spine Diaphram

8   Spine Waist

9   Spine Lumbar

10   Intestinal track

11   Left Kidney

12   Sub-conscious
      mind

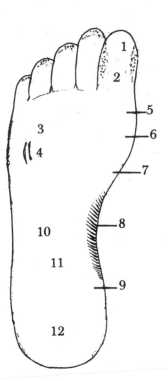

numbers 5,6,7,8,9 are areas   LEFT
in spine in line with the
throat etc.

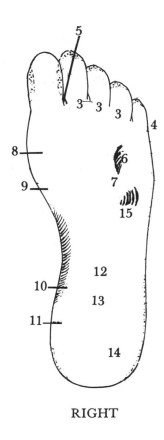

RIGHT

1	Pituitary Gland
2	Thyroid
3	Sinus
4	Ears
5	Eyes
6	Liver
7	Gall Bladder
8	Spine Base Neck
9	Opposite Heart
10	Waist
11	Lumbar
12	Stomach
13	R. Kidney
14	Sub-conscious mind
15	Lung

protected by shoes. The diagrams show the points of
sensitivity which relate to the various organs in the
body, and by pressing on these points either with
the knuckle of a finger or with a rubber point of a
pencil, the Healer can locate the organs in the body
which are not receiving the degree of life-force necessary to maintain good health.

These pain areas are caused by crystalline deposits
forming at the nerve endings and when these are
pressed they hurt "like a needle pricking" as patients
will describe the pain felt.

Then normal healing techniques can be used in
order to restore the life force to the area concerned.
Generally, after a treatment or two, the pain leaves
the area of the foot as it has gone from the bodily
organ to which the nerve relates.

Practicing with a friend will confirm how remarkably accurate this form of diagnosis can be, and the
Healer can quickly familiarize himself with the various locations by remembering that the organs on
the right side of the body reflect in the right foot and
the reverse on the left foot, e.g., the liver would be
on the right foot and the heart on the left, whereas
the eyes will reflect on both feet just inside the bottom
part of the big toe.

Healing Techniques

(See Illustrations pp. 136-141)
1. Position # 1
    Healer holding wrists of patient.
    Note the healer's hands on wrist of patient and
that knees touch healer's knees. The healer's knees

are on the outside, thus, making a circuit for the positive current of the healer's hand and knee to be in touch with the corresponding polarities of the patient, i.e., positive to negative, right to left.

This process insures a complete healing circuit set up throughout the body. It is interesting to note that this power is resisted by persons who are heavily under the influence of drugs or vitamins.

2. Position # 2

Healer standing behind seated patient — hand on patient's head.

Note healer's hand on either side of head. The healer remains in position until he feels power entering the patient's head at maximum capacity.

3. Position # 3

(2 Persons)

Male healer sitting in front with female healer holding head of patient with hands making contact with the 12 cranial nerves, but avoiding the chakra at crown of head where life force enters body, i.e., the coronel chakra.

The male power is generally more impulsive like the kick of a mule, while the female is deeper, gentler, and frequently more penetrative in such sensitive areas as the eyes and ears.

It is possible for two healers to ''cross powers'' whereby they both channel power through the coronel chakra of the partner. This is effective with any two healers, i.e., both male and/or female, and this prevents any healer from feeling other than great happiness when the patient may comment to the partner that his hands are "full of power tonight," because they are both giving to one another.

The healers will arrange which of the instructions listed to share for each partner, bearing in mind that it is seldom necessary for any treatment to last longer than 20-30 minutes. Of course, treatment is quicker with two healers than with one.

4. Position #4

Healer stands to the right side of patient with right hand on forehead, left hand at base of neck, which permits the healing force to make contact with the pineal gland and commences to transmit to pituitary gland in the same area.

5. Position #5

Healer moves to left side of patient placing left hand on forehead, right hand at base of neck. Then he waits until power is stronger at base of neck than at forehead.

6. Position #6

Healer places hands on shoulders of patient, with both thumbs on either side of lower cervical ganglion. Thumbs should be nearly touching; this position brought about by healer standing directly behind the patient's chair.

7. Position #7

Healer places left hand over thyroid gland and heart area (over throat chakra), with right hand on spine at shoulder level. Make figure 8 with the flat of right hand moving from one side of body to the other, from top to bottom. This is a wonderfully effective way of activating the motor and sensory nerves of the entire spine. (The center of the figure 8 is on the spine itself.)

8. Position #8

Healer now moves chair to the right side of patient's body and places his right hand over the solar plexus and left hand approximately over kidney area. Thus, it frees, or commences to free some of the tensions and blockages caught up in solar plexus area, which is sometimes called the seat of the mechanical brain, by which Rev. Street has found to be partly linked with the subconscious mind itself.

9. Position #9

Now the healing force has been brought through the body and, with the exception of the extremities, most areas have been influenced. Healer may now treat directly the sick area, i.e., the ulcer, asthma, etc., with right hand over the sick part. If possible, the left hand should be over the opposite side of the body to insure transmission.

10. Position #10

After the healer feels that the part has been sufficiently treated in #8, he can finalize the transmission of the healing force by "combing" the arms and legs of patient with fingertips of both hands, commencing left, right — from shoulders to fingertips and thighs to toes.

11. Position #11

This is the same as #3 with two assistant healers on either side with hands placed on top of shoulders of both patient and healer. In fact, the three healers, to side and front of patient are virtually power stations; and an added power boost can be obtained from this position.

The fourth healer behind the patient will do most of the work as far as hand movements and treatments of specific areas of the body are concerned.

NOTE CAREFULLY: The time spent in different positions varies with the patient's size and age. It is unwise to overtreat an elderly person or a child. Much less time is required in such cases.

Clairvoyant Diagnosis

As the healer becomes attuned in consciousness to Spirit, he will generally receive psychic directions which may register as impressions or specific pictures as to the area of illness, and frequently its origin. This faculty may not necessarily be given to a person possessing healing power. But maybe with someone else associated with him.

Need Precedes Healing Rays

In an experiment with heat and healing, slides were used to try to register healing power. The hands of Harry Edwards, the well-known English healer, were tested by a thermometer while he was treating a patient, and no change in temperature took place.

Then a group of English healers used Dutch lenses which were said to register healing rays, but this attempt also failed.

The failure was continual with the healers as they worked on each other, but they found that as soon as a patient who was actually ill sat down for treatment, the healing rays began and showed on the film. The difference was in the fact that a definite need existed.

HEALING POSITIONS

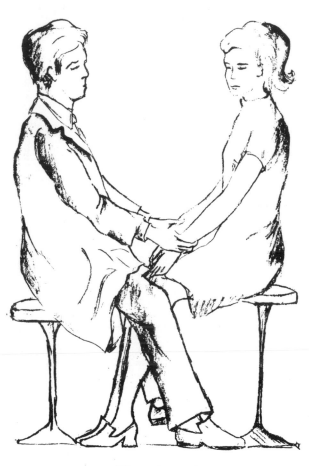

(Illustration #1)

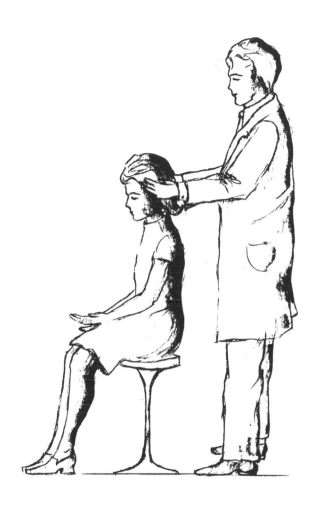

(Illustration #2)

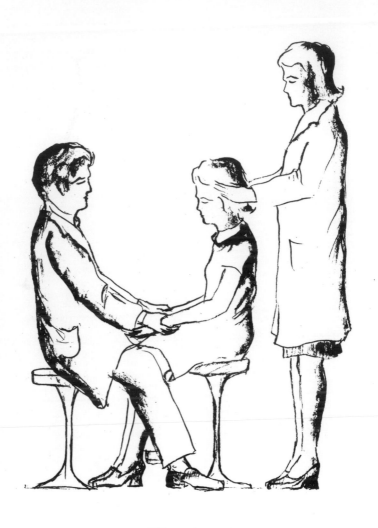

(Illustration #3)

(Illustration #4)

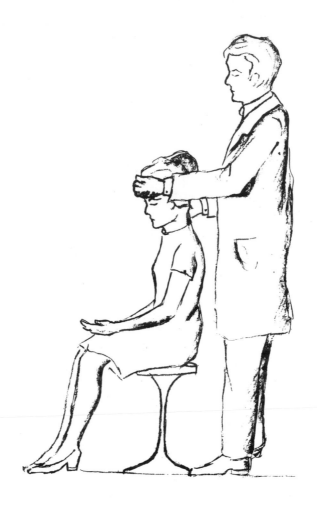

(Illustration #5)

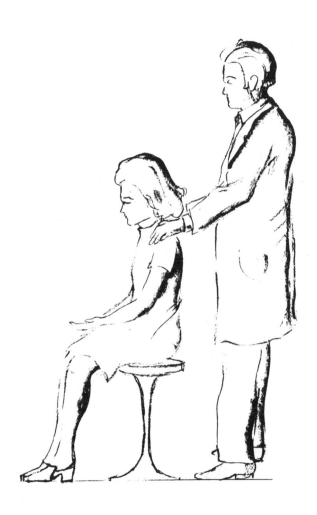

(Illustration #6)

(Illustration #7)

(Illustration #8)

(Illustration #9)

(Illustration #10)

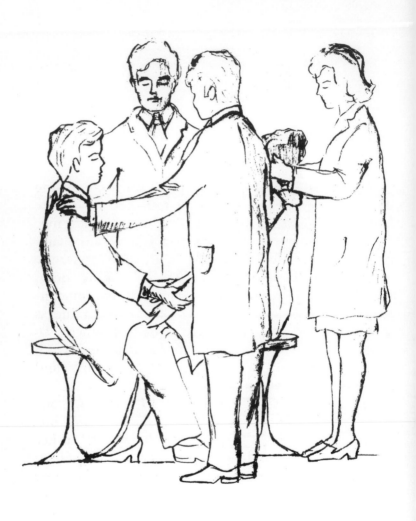

(Illustration #11)

Chapter 12

Healing from the Patient's Point of View

The most important factor in all spiritual healing is that the sufferer wants to be well and to be free from any illness from which he may be suffering. Lest this statement seem too trite, there are many persons whose illness either attracts another family member to them or gives them a talking point which would otherwise be absent. In the subconscious mind of such persons, the fact of their illness is firmly fixed and considered to be permanent, so that no healer can transmute the malady into health unless it is with the permission, both consciously and subconsciously, of the patient.

Take, for example, a mother who has but one child left of a family — divorced, lonely, and unhappy. She feels that her daughter "owes it" to her to be a companion. It is very difficult to suggest to the mother that she take on a job or undertake some occupation which will give her an opportunity to think about others and not herself. Generally, these people become very introspective and subconsciously caught up in the self. So the first key is for the person to want to be separated from the illness.

Remaining Calm before Treatment

Since most patients do not fall within that category and have a genuine illness which they do not want, it is well for them to be relaxed and passive when they come for the healing session. It is also important that they be as absorbent and receptive to the healing power of Spirit as possible. Otherwise, an over-anxious state can be obstructive and present a barrier in healing.

Uniting Desire

Thus, the patient combines his will with that of the healer in order to allow the fullest flow of power from the Spirit which heals.

Medical histories are not particularly important to the healer, as he will prefer to diagnose the current illness and set about treating it. As a rule, a casebook is kept wherein the healer records certain impressions which he feels are important.

Sometimes the cause of the blockage or illness may readily be perceived. Frequently, a dramatic relief is obtained which permits the life-force to become reactivated, sometimes instantaneously.

It is usual for a patient to see a healer about once a week; sometimes two visits a week can be helpful if an opportunity allows. However, should the patient desire to return for another treatment, it is he who must ask the healer for help.

Chapter 13

Kundalini and Sex

The Kundalini or "serpent fire" is, in fact, the creative essence of our bodies and manifests as the source of the sex impulse. It resides in the sacral chakra where it lies coiled like a serpent and waits for the spiritual impulse of the aspirant to direct it on its journey upwards.

This energy is provided by a positive and a negative current which permits the power of the Kundalini to become raised as it journeys via an etheric canal in the center of the spine called the *Sushuma nadi,* and it makes contact with the dormant psychic centers or chakras. As the Kundalini power becomes awakened, the first chakra at the base of the spine begins to become illumined and the aspirant develops a spiritual consciousness.

The second center in the spine is opposite the navel and when vivified, the aspirant is able to journey on the astral plane; some experiences on this plane may return to him in his ordinary waking consciousness, and some will be hidden temporarily in order to see how he progressess further.

As the power continues to the center in the solar plexus, (which is the sun center of the human body), there develops a new energy of a spiritual kind; this awakening makes possible certain forms of physical mediumship including the movement of trumpets, speaking in tongues, and various subconscious activities of a psychic kind.

As the power continues its journey, contact is made with the heart center where Christ Consciousness is seated, and herein are the wisdom and love qualities.

As the power proceeds to the throat center, the gift of clairaudience is stirred within the person concerned. The psychic faculties of many singers have been opened abnormally in that chakra due to the use of the voice.

Proceeding upwards, the force then makes contact with the brow chakra and bestows clairvoyant vision on the aspirant. Continuing development of the pineal gland is said to resemble a lotus flower which has its seed within the head itself. But its flower is discernible outside and above the head, so that with development, a state of cosmic consciousness can be attained.

Danger in Forcing Development

Premature awakening of the Kundalini force is dangerous and should never be attempted by any seeker after divine truth, because it will surely lead him into distressing situations over which he has no control.

The reader may be asking, "Where can I go to get this power or development?" He may be sure that the ancient adage applies here: "When the pupil is ready, the Teacher will appear." And this truth most certainly is applicable to him for as he unselfishly seeks to serve his Brother Man, spirit intelligences will be watching over his progress. Ultimately, he will be given every encouragement and help possible.

There are also seven negative chakras which can be awakened, but these locations are never passed on in writing. Knowledge of them is normally not important unless one is interested in developing occult powers of an entirely different nature than are used in psychic healing. Naturally, it is the sincere desire of the healer to bring comfort into the lives of other people.

The Sex Force

The sex force is, indeed, the most potent of all powers and also can be the most damaging in the lives of persons living on our planet today, because it is so little understood.

Whereas sex can be the most beautiful and gratifying force given to God's children, it can also be the means of producing great agony and problems of a kind which can ruin lives in both social, political, and spiritual ways. It is, perhaps, the force which makes the spiritual aspirant most vulnerable. Undoubtedly, he must have complete control over it before the spiritual forces can confidently use him as a channel. We are always attacked at our weak spots, and if sex happens to be one of them, then we will very soon become enmeshed in its web. This weakness will prevent our making further progress, as well as retard our spiritual development, creating a reaction to our activities in this area.

It is not necessarily true to say that a person

leading a celibate life is any more or less developed
than a person who is a parent, but if we are able to
poooooo nothing   not even the desire for sex — we
are becoming free of physical entanglements. Ultimately, we will be required to separate ourselves from
all 'things' in order to become spiritually free.

In India, the yogis are sometimes referred to as
"household yogis," when they have a family and
enjoy a formal home life. There are also the yogis
who lead celibate lives, but it is difficult to say that
one is in a state of deeper grace than the other. So
much depends on our karma in this area and the
lessons which we are required to learn.

"Creating" Homosexuality

Perhaps the idea is not generally known, but Rev.
Street believes that a direct link exists between abnormal gene defects in an infant and the mother's
desire for a certain-sexed child. It is thought that
the mother's intensity of thought on this forthcoming
birth can be extremely disturbing to the fetus. Should
the child be of the opposite sex than that which she
wants, the male-female genes can become disturbed,
thus, giving rise to homosexual behavior in the
newly-created individual. Such an occurrence may
affect the child's development into adulthood.

The Maori people in New Zealand and many of
the other ancient races never fall into this error of
thinking. Expectant mothers will never comment that
they are hoping for a certain-sexed child to be born,
because they know that this abnormal development
can take place. So if one directly asks the mother

whether she wants a boy or a girl, she will laughingly say, "Whatever God gives me."

It is interesting to note that the Maoris have no homosexuals among their people.

Prayer Before Sex

Since many marriages do not enjoy a happy sex relationship, Rev. Street suggests that the offering of a prayer of blessing before the forthcoming sex act can be of great value. Praying that the experience may be enjoyable for the partner is an extremely potent way of bringing Spirit into matter. The same divine descension occurs when saying grace before a meal, asking a prayer of blessing on someone, or seeking a state of protection before sleep. But this measure is seldom initiated before the sexual experience.

Of course, this prayer can be said in silence without the partner's knowing anything about it, or if a state of spiritual union exists between the partners concerned, then the prayer is enhanced when said aloud.

Offering the Self to God

When Rev. Street was in Sydney on one occasion, he met a fine-looking chap in his early 20's who was experiencing great homosexual difficulties. Returning to Sydney several years later, he met the young man again and found that he had become a priest. He was radiant, glowing with a certain quality which

was not there before, and Rev. Street asked him what
had changed his life.

"Well, I was lacking a great deal of freedom in the
'gay' life I was leading," he said. "And one morning
I was just walking along the pavement and offered
to God that one thing which was most precious in my
life — sex. Then the power was transmuted to adoration and love of God, and I became free and was
able to start to train for the priesthood!"

This story illustrates the need for all spiritual
seekers to be familiar with the Law of Renunciation,
or "the Law of Flow" which is in three parts: (1)
As we give, so we receive; (2) As we receive, so we
continue to give, until finally we are holding nothing
and are prepared to possess nothing; (3) Finally,
we are free of all possessions, having given everything to God.

Even as the young man in Sydney gave up that
thing which was most precious to him, he found a
tremendous joy and freedom coming from Spirit as
compensatory blessing. To anyone who is willing
to release possessions in his life, his whole being
will be suffused with radiance.

Thus, having removed those things which were
most important, a strange part of the law is often
in evidence; once we have made the decision to be
free from something, usually God does not require
us to give it up. But we must be prepared to do so
first.

In other words, we are not holding anything and
are living in accordance with the Law of Flow, which
permits things to pass through us to other people.
It is a wonderful heritage which places us completely

within the knowledge that God is sole Creator and the supplier of abundance for our needs; He is our Father. Also, co-equal is God the Mother, the Sustainer who loves and influences our activities in a continuous and sustaining manner. To hear a soul address his Lord as "Dear Father-Mother God . . .," one quickly senses the beauty and the love of our true parentage as His Children.

Chapter 14

Magnetism, Hypnosis, Security While Asleep

Magnetism is the attraction of the mind to some force which is almost irresistible to the individual. It can take the form of drugs, alcohol, money, sex, power, domination over another person's mind, or many other ways, but its force will be a test for every spiritual aspirant until he has obtained freedom from its power.

It is very easy to criticize someone else who smokes or takes alcohol in excess or is controlled by something over which we ourselves have gained mastery. But it is prudent to remember that we are always hit at our weak spots in one life or another, and frequently, a person may find it very difficult to break something which he may quite well have emphasized in an earlier life.

The possibility certainly does exist of one person gaining control over another's mind by occult means or by hypnotic techniques. One day in New Zealand, Rev. Street was about to address a meeting, and as the people arrived he noticed two persons in the audience who were obviously controlled by someone else. Therefore, he commented that he had noticed several persons present who were being influenced by someone else, and should they care to make contact with him for help, he would be available at a certain hotel the next day. To his astonishment, not two, but four people came, and as it happened they were all controlled by the same magician who was practicing his powers in the area.

Breaking the Influence

When an individual is controlled in such a manner, he can find it quite easy to break the influence, provided he sincerely desires to do so.

For example, suppose a person is over-influencing your life and using methods which you know have forced you into a situation where you do not want to be. To remedy this problem, practice holding his face in your mind and making a white cross over him; this procedure allows the spirit of Christ within you to bless the spirit of Christ within him. Quickly, the hold will change, because you have placed a mental force or an occult power onto the highest possible spiritual level of which you are capable and are imparting only love to the person concerned. So any influence which has been used over you will be broken automatically, provided you have the will to make the initial break.

In accordance with the Law of Flow, we are wise to be detached from everything and everyone in order to know complete freedom. Then — and only then — are we able to move with spiritual security in accordance with God's will and not our own.

Should you happen to be in the presence of one from whom you feel, perhaps, a sex force emanating, or possibly a person who wishes to gain control over you, it is very simple to break these attachments.

If the force be that of sex or some other magnetic power, simply make a cross from your mind right over the person. A white cross is easy to make and very effective, as it will immediately transmute any force emanating from him or her into a spiritual love. The power of your own Christ will relate to the same Spirit within the other individual, eliminating all other power. In this connection, it is good to remember that we can love everybody, even though there may be some things about him which we do not like.

Another effective method to use with a person who is seeking to hypnotize you against your will is to make a black speck between his eyes and concentrate on it with the affirmation, "You are simply a little black speck in the universe, trying to gain control over my mind." This statement will immediately neutralize any adverse mental powers of the other person.

It is strange to think that by using these simple techniques, any influence employed even by persons in high offices — civil, commercial, or spiritual — can be neutralized in the twinkling of an eye. No word need ever be said, nor anyone else conscious of what is taking place, except you. The Psalm of Gita so beautifully states: "Man has been given dominion over everything that God has made, and all things have been placed beneath his feet."

Rev. Street tells the story of an actress in London who was developing a stutter, because men would accost her on the way back to her apartment after a show in the evening. Finally, she went to see him for counseling, and that very evening, someone ap-

proached her! Using the above technique which she
had learned, within seconds the man had apologized
for disturbing her. As she regained her composure,
she allowed him to walk her home safely. It is interesting that she had no more trouble thereafter.

Antagonism

Should a strong personality conflict exist, perhaps
in your home, or maybe in your marriage, the same
technique using the white cross over the person will
bring an immediate change. The angry words being
aimed at you will simply become hot air, or the
tears — merely hot water. This act will in no way
affect the love which you feel towards the person's
spirit which is within you.

Of course, for the person who is not following the
Christian faith, a simple alteration in the symbol used
is just as effective as the cross.

The Dweller on the Threshold

As we grow spiritually, each of us is confronted
with tests which we must overcome. As these individual battles are fought and finally won, so then the
Dweller on the Threshold opens yet another door to
permit our entry into deeper spiritual awareness. This
"dweller" is, in truth, the guardian of our utmost
spiritual happiness and growth. Even as we overcome the negative features which attack us (until ultimately we have become free of them all), there will
also be a tremendous compensatory joy forthcoming.
This experience will far exceed any benefit or hap-

piness which we would have gained from taking advantage of the opportunities afforded to our lower nature, over which we have gained control.

Security While Asleep

We must never neglect our development by concentrating totally on the activities of the day, for we should also *sleep* knowing that we are perfectly secure. Too often, individuals do not realize the necessity of safeguarding themselves and family from astral attack or psychic disturbance during the night.

Because it is not a particularly difficult matter to contact another person's sleeping mind, or even to occupy the body in a physical sense, a security against such intrusions should be put up during sleep. This simple method is enacted by praying for security, both for yourself and for all members of the family. Otherwise, they can quite easily be attacked even if we ourselves are immune or invulnerable. It is the spiritual light that provides our etheric bodies with a protective cover or armor.

Therefore, before retiring, let our final prayer take a form such as: "May the Guardian Angels of Jesus Christ watch over us while we sleep." And as you mention the name of each person for whom you pray, picture his face in your mind for a moment, until all persons have been included — yourself being last on the list. This practice must be utilized each night in order to sleep in adequate security.*

---

* Should the reader care to know more of this subject, see Noel Street's book, DREAMER AWAKE!, available from the Lotus Ashram in Miami, $3.00 postpaid.

Psychic Self-Defense

A final method which is quite useful in breaking another person's influence over you is simply by "disconnecting" your eyes from his. There will be an immediate breaking of the psychic force of light emanating through the eyes.

Thus, equipped with an etheric armor which is · both protective and helpful in spiritual development, the aspirant can safely move into groups of other persons. His growth is assured as he seeks to express love on the highest spiritual level, spreading light into the lives of his Brother Man — through service.

A bronze statue presented to Noel Street — an appreciation
from a healing and meditation group he formed in Melbourne
Australia 1965.

SECTION III

THE APPLICATION OF HEALING POWER

Chapter 15

The Power of Love

How much do you love? What is your true capacity to love others and yourself? Upon pondering this question in depth, one can begin to realize quite readily its relevance in the area of health and happiness.

Have you ever known anyone who is constantly using his energy to hate everyone around him? Usually at the core of this person is hidden the face of discontentment with self, often a glaring projection of self-hate aimed at anyone else in range.

If we could all stop and realize how this emotion works against us to break us down — quite easily through the physical body — we might think twice before allowing such negativity to control us at times.

Once I knew a man who had spent many years in a rage. As time passed, he appeared more disgruntled with job, family, and life in general. Little things would throw him into a rampage, and he must have been rather difficult to live with. Finally, he suffered a severe heart attack.

For three weeks the doctors had little hope for his recovery, but gradually he began to respond and grow stronger. At last, the day came when a full rehabilitation program was planned for him, and the first item on the list related to his emotions.

"Mr. Miller, you must attempt to stay calm and relaxed," was the admonition, as this factor was vital for his maintenance of better health.

Of course, to change a whole life pattern of grumbling was not an easy task. But the patient obviously did his "homework," for now he compliments his daily walk with a genuine smile at neighbors and friends, and the direct compensation is better health than he has ever had.

The Love-Hate Continuum

What is the relationship of love to hate? Rev. Street explained this question to me in an interesting manner.

"Suppose," he said, "we combine these two emotions on a scale of + 10 and -10. Now, let us consider the fact that we have a certain amount of energy to utilize which is rated at 10 points, either above or below, love and hate respectively. In this way, we can see how we use our energy, directing it above into the positive area of love, or below into the negative area of hate."

In other words, our love-hate capacity is fastened to a scale of energy, and our own will is the control which directs the needle. Thus, it is easy to understand how an individual can passionately expose his dual nature on an issue. One day he feels great love for someone, and the next day the object of his affection is receiving an equal reverse of sentiment.

The Cosmic Link

The inevitable effect of hate links us to a person with whom we usually do not desire an association.

When that person has aroused anger or a feeling of animosity in us, then ultimately, he has gained some degree of control over us. Take, for example, the employer who does something which invokes a negative response in his employee. Whatever the justification the worker feels in "returning the blow," the truth of the matter is that the employer has some degree of power which manifests in the need of the employees to reciprocate. So the real secret in the situation, whatever it may be, is *not to react.* When this state of neutrality can prevail, then the next step is a replacement of hate with love, or redirecting destructive energy into constructive energy.

Perhaps one may think, "Well, 'ole Bill really doesn't deserve my kindness!" It may be true that one has wronged us unduly; the world and its people are often in the wrong, but our negative reaction will not change them. One thing is sure, however — a law is established that whatever we send out into the ethers will return to us sooner or later. Even if only out of self-defense, we should want to send out those positive qualities. We need to understand this principle in depth. Otherwise, we shall suffer the consequences of the hate which we harbor in our hearts.

"Love Thy Neighbor. . . ."

The verse in the Scriptures, "Love thy neighbor as thyself. . . ." implies that the love which we have for ourselves will directly relate to the love which will flow out to those around us. Is it really possible to love others if we are lacking in love for ourselves?

I have a friend named Peter who grew up with the

belief that he was not loved. Being a child in a
"orphan's home," the very phrase had gnawed at
him as long as he could remember. His recompense
to the world was a tough exterior which spoke of
self-sufficiency and mocked people's kindness to him.
Beneath the facade was, at best, a lonely boy who
craved love and security.

As he began to awaken spiritually in his adulthood, he was able to bring into his consciousness
the truth that there are, in reality, no "orphans."
We are all equally loved and valued by our Father-
Mother God. With this new realization, Peter began
to draw up the true spiritual love which had always
been within him, waiting for an opportunity to express
itself. Now, he can truly love himself in the right per-
spective and extend it to those around him, which
he does in full measure today.

Returning Good for Evil

As we walk the spiritual Pathway, the real test
comes with the command: "Do unto others as you
would them do unto you. . . ." given by our Master
Christ.

Putting aside self-justification in any form, there
are several steps we can take in seeking to become
more loving.

(1) Pray for that person to whom you feel a slight
resentment or an active hate. As you direct your
prayers to him for his good, you automatically remove yourself from the center of the situation, and
any negative ties are relinquished.

Now pray for yourself that the Christ love will fill your heart, for the good of the universe. Ask, knowing that the Father withholds nothing good from His Children.

(2) See that opposing person as Spirit. See yourself as Spirit.

As we develop into a state of cosmic consciousness, we realize that our true spiritual selves are not composed of emotion, mind, or the physical components. In truth, we are not a part of the circumstances around us. In this knowledge, we can truly live on a level above the physical world, partaking of our spiritual heritage.

(3) An effective technique which Rev. Street teaches in his classes relates to the clearing of the subconscious mind. As our minds become cluttered with petty grievances and resentments, the flow of spiritual love is blocked, and the effect on the subconscious mind can be stupendous.

Perhaps we have wanted to be free completely from an old relationship which keeps emerging from the subconscious. To bring about a change, think of that person who has harmed you or whom you have harmed; at night before you sleep, picture him in your mind's eye and project a white cross over him.

This simple effort will raise the Christ love in you, as it also brings forth the Christ love in him. The effect will be amazing, as the shackles in the subconscious are loosed and perfect freedom comes to the aspirant. This experience is healing in its purest form!

To Love and Be Loved

As human beings we are made in the image of God, possessing the capacity to love and the need to be loved. As a child, I often wondered why God had gone to so much trouble to make us. What was in His mind as He breathed the breath of life into His Children and called us each by name?

My concern with this question seemed to lodge on the belief that He wanted someone to love. So out of the depths of Himself, He measured a generous portion of Love into this creation. As an inheritance, we reap the joys of God incarnate — returning that love to Him with our lives. Furthermore, we have the opportunity to send love out into the world and see it transform and change consciousness.

Everybody's Grandma

To illustrate this point, let me tell you about a friend named John. Being my counselor and friend, I was able to observe the tremendous capacity to love that this man possessed in abundance. Observing the resultant healing power which affected so many people who came his way, I one day asked if he had ever had any relationship which presented difficulty for him.

He thought for a moment and then the familiar twinkle came into his eyes. "My grandma was the biggest challenge of my life!" he laughed.

"She was the most cantankerous woman I ever knew and continually blamed everyone for her own problems," he recounted.

Because John had a job which required travel, he was out of town for fairly long periods at a time. Invariably, upon returning to his hometown, he would find that the grandmother had packed up her belongings and moved from the last known address. This irrational behavior was due partly to oncoming senility, spurred by an unreasonable self-will.

On locating her whereabouts, the old woman would loudly protest to John, saying that he did not care about her; otherwise, he would not go away so often and leave her alone. After all, she had no one else to look after her.

With great patience, he would attempt to get her settled down before he was required to make another trip for his company. Without fail, the same situation would recur as soon as he was gone.

At last, he found it necessary to place her in a nursing home where she could be properly cared for. On return trips, John would visit the lonely old woman, sitting hour after hour with her as she complained of her circumstances. Without a need to retaliate, he would quietly listen, patting her hand and sending a flow of spiritual love to her as she sat before him growing increasingly disgruntled.

Gradually, however, John began to observe a very slight change in the grandmother. She would almost smile when he went to see her, and after many months she became quieter and a bit more peaceful.

One day while working in a distant town, John received a telephone call to come quickly as the relative was dying. On reaching the hospital, the nurses explained that she had been in a semi-conscious state for several hours and had called for him at intervals. As he reached her bedside, a faint flicker of recognition dawned on the wrinkled old face and she reached out her hand to him and smiled feebly. Several hours later she died.

John's story truly unveiled to me the power of love. He went on to say that we all have a 'grandmother' in our lives. If we utilize our inherent capacity to love, lives will be changed for the better. Indeed, no love that is ever sent out into the universe is lost!

Chapter 16

The Development of Cosmic Consciousness

The earlier chapter on meditation provided a pathway into unexplored light wherein we were able to bring the consciousness into a vibrational rate, transcending normal thought. When drawn into the realms of the "Silence," we become more attuned to the voice of the Spirit.

This communication is sometimes referred to as the "peace which passes understanding."

After practicing this form of meditation for a few days or a few weeks (depending on how long the individual requires), until all the colors are seen with equal luminosity and until a state of requisite stillness is obtained, transmissions will occur from the world of spirit directed by our teachers and helpers, or if you prefer, from enlightenment itself.

Be this as it may, the fact remains that we are in touch with the source which is beyond our normal range of consciousness. The vibration is distinctively different, which is the potentially transforming link in our lives. As our dreams alter, so too, will our thinking process become kinder, more understanding, and our whole nature will become softer and more beautiful.

171

A Warning

In the midst of this new language that is being taught to us, we must heed the vital warning of over-rating our own importance. At first, the communications will be accurate and of utmost benefit in our living, so that we may regard this experience as one which separates us from our fellows. In this attitude, we err — the occurrence has been only an initial training period for the development of our spiritual consciousness. This gift has been extended to us from intelligences greater than our own, and they are attempting to aid us in development so that we will be of greater use in service to our Brother Man. It is, indeed, more than a mere extrasensory appendage which will ultimately benefit only ourselves.

The Trend Toward Cosmic Consciousness

It is obvious that today's world is thinking in terms of enlarged and cosmic relationships rather than the by-gone functionings in a small area of activity. So too, standard methods are available to us for expanding our own consciousness onto a larger scale of thought, in keeping with this trend. This alteration calls for a forfeit of the individual facets of our personality, so that our personal growth can make room for cosmic awareness. As a result, the brilliance of our new light will glow with universal value.

Only the self can stand in the way of this prospect, for the exciting period of early development will soon end beyond our control. The experience has served merely to clear away the debris of an earthly life, so that spiritual light can begin to flow through us as a reflectory benefit to others.

At this point, let us ask the question: "Are we seeking to become servants or masters?" Our Lord referred to the question of superiority among disciples — "Unless ye become as little children, ye cannot enter the kingdom of heaven." And this truth is the essence of our growth: as transmitters of spiritual light and servants of God, are we able to carry out the instructions which are imparted to us and finally follow up these conveyances with action?

Jonah and the Whale

We are all familiar with the direction which Jonah received to go to Ninevah and how he avoided this difficult message by boarding a ship instead. Afterwards, he spent three days in the belly of a whale, until he was given another chance and did accomplish that task which he was originally asked to do.

And so the story runs with our own self-development. Anyone can unfold into a state of cosmic consciousness, provided he is not seeking self-aggrandizement. Exactly how is this heightened spiritual state reached? What is the actual process that brings this enlightenment to our consciousness?

"Where Wast Thou . . .?"

As we search the pages of spiritual history, various forms of the answer appear to us. In truth, we are eternal beings. The Egyptian Book of the Dead which was written some 5,000 years before Christ by unknown hands, contains this lovely stanza: "Infinite time without beginning and without end, I inherit eternity and everlastingness is part of me."

Again, this thought is reproduced in the Book of Job, 38:4. "Where wast thou when I laid the foundations of the earth? When the morning stars sang together, and the sons of God shouted for joy? Answer if thou hast the understanding."

Surely, too, we have pondered this ageless question. Where were we when light first shone onto our planet? We find the answer written some hundreds of years later in Proverbs 8:22-30. "The Lord possessed me in the beginning of His way, before His works ruled. Then I was by Him as one brought up with him, and I was daily His delight, rejoicing always before Him."

Citizens of Eternity

If, then, we feel sure that we are truly Citizens of Eternity, we must be aware of the long series of lessons which we have had to learn as a result of meeting our Brother Man in various guises and difficulties.

How beneficial to our progress would be the consciousness that is not bound by individual thought or egoic selfhood! The following meditative technique will enable us to develop a state of illumination which will be life-changing in that respect.

Advanced Method

Continuing the method thus laid out, we sit quietly in a chair, conscious of the different colors or vibrational rates which have been expressed in our consciousness. In a state of stillness, our spiritual love and adoration flows out to our Master.

Now, in order to still the mind further, we can slowly affirm in silence: (1) I am not the body, (2) I am not the mind, (3) I am not the emotions, (4) I am one with God. Then allow the consciousness to focus on a star on the very distant horizon — as far away as can be visualized. With the depth of the soul, know that the light of God is within and that there was a time when you first came forth, even as a spark of the divine flame. We can feel that star as being our own spiritual soul or self.

Identifying with the light, affirm: "I am that star, that star am I." Feel blended into light in a total cosmic sense, leaving no thought for self but only one of unity with the Father-Mother God.

Practicing this technique ten to fifteen minutes daily will lead to an inexpressible peace, as the conveyances from Spirit will enlarge our nature. A feeling of progress will come into our consciousness, as we become more receptive to the voice of Spirit and less to our own desire to gain something from meditation. It is wise to remember that Spirit comes to mind, and mind does not normally go to Spirit.

A Step Toward Dual-Consciousness

In this ADVANCED TECHNIQUE, it is vital to realize that we have entered a state of timeless cosmic attunement. In this moment, we are developing dual consciousness instead of going into trance. This

state permits a complete and absolute control over
our own mind by way of the spiritual will.

So when we feel that we have been in this state of
exalted awareness long enough, we simply return to
our normal mind — without any stress or strain —
by willing the mind to re-occupy the kneeling form
before the altar, which was developed in the first stage
of our meditation. At this point, we gently and quietly
descend the steps of light to our normal state of
being.

The time in the Silence will vary and will depend
largely on the need for being there. Practice makes
perfect, and some aspirants may need more practice
than others.

Spreading the Light

In this form of psychic development, we have indeed, become Citizens of Eternity, and the light of
God will flow through us in an ever-increasing out-
pouring. Undoubtedly, your light will fill the dark
places of the earth, and God's healing love will flow
freely to His Children — channeled through you,
His faithful servant.

"INTO LIGHT"

Bronze Sculpture by Mirtala Bentov

Mirtala Bentov makes her sculptures directly in wax and casts them by the lost wax process. Her studio is in Wayland, Massachusetts.

Chapter 17

Psychic Healing on ALL Levels:
Physical, Mental, Spiritual, Absent, During Sleep

Healing on the Physical Level

Noel Street began his healing ministry without any intention of continuing. After working with Leslie Symons in the healing clinic for awhile, the time came when his first patient approached him alone. It was on a Saturday night, and a woman came knocking on his door asking for treatment. It seemed that she was having a dreadful time with ulcers in her eyes, and her physician could not be reached over the weekend. In desperation, she sought this healer of whom she had heard.

Not really knowing what would happen, the man invited her in and placed his hands over her eyes rendering the best aid that he could. Within minutes, the patient exclaimed that the pain was gone. Amazed at this occurrence, Noel realized that Spirit had used him as a channel for healing power. The next morning a phone call revealed that the pain was not only gone, but the ulcers as well!

Questioning him about these happenings, the healer explained to me that each time he places his hands on a patient to treat for a physical disease, he never really knows what the outcome of the treatment will be. But there can be no greater pleasure for a healer than for a patient to respond and become much better.

A Desire for Good Health

Of course, healing is a two-way street. The desire of the patient to be restored to health goes hand in hand with healing treatment.

Many of Rev. Street's patients are advised on diet and exercise when they come for treatment. This approach is one which helps to maintain good health after treatment is received, and most people gratefully take the suggestions offered and use them to their own advantage. However, a small percentage is never quite willing to "work" for better health; instead, they want it all done for them in the twinkling of an eye by the doctor or healer.

Recently in Dallas, a woman telephoned to make an appointment with Rev. Street. When I asked how he could help her, she seemed a bit undecided in why she wanted to come. Finally, she announced that she thought she might like to come for a healing treatment.

When she arrived all wide-eyed and anxious, I must say I had my doubts about her interest in healing, as there seem to be a few would-be psychics who are lured more by Rev. Street's clairvoyant abilities than by any hope of making their lives more open spiritually.

As the woman was received into the healing room by the healer, I returned to the office. Within minutes, the door flew open and out shot the woman in a huff, looking neither left nor right and slamming the door behind her!

Very shortly thereafter, a telephone call from this patient unveiled the nature of the unrest.

"Miss Dupree," boomed the voice on the other end, "I just wanted to tell you that I didn't give you a donation for that treatment, because I wasn't healed! If Rev. Street 'advertizes' to be a healer, then that is what he should do! *Instant* healing is what I wanted, and instead he began to tell me what I should eat and not eat! So if I get healed, I'll send you a donation, but not until!" And down went the receiver with a jar!

Wondering what that was all about, I was quite well-acquainted with my friend's method of advising on diet and exercise to compliment the healing process. As it happened, I found that the woman had been disappointed because she had hoped the healer would exhibit some of his psychic "tricks," and when he had refused to tell her fortune, she angrily aired her resentments in this manner.

We had a good laugh over the situation, as it was a direct insight into human nature. But for the most part, people who come for healing treatment are sincere and desirous of help, which they usually receive in full measure.

Healing on the Mental Level

It is possible for the healer to be a very effective channel to a person who is suffering from a mental illness or disturbance, provided he continues to relate by his spirit consciousness to the mind of the patient concerned. Attunement is made and treatment given to specific areas in the head itself.

This kind of psychic healing is performed on a spiritual level only, not on a mental level; otherwise, a state of mind influencing mind develops, and this area is well taken care of by psychiatrists and hypnotists.

It must be clearly understood at this point that psychic healing on a mental level refers to that group of individuals which is suffering from an obsession of the mind. The expression of such an obsession in the personality shows itself in various shapes and forms, but usually the end result is an imbalance in the mental body wherein the person directs most of his mental energy toward satisfying a craving of some kind.

A good example of a mental obsession for a physical craving is the picture of an active alcoholic whose sole thought is directed toward where the next drink will come from. If one has ever witnessed or experienced the suffering of such a person who has the disease of alcoholism, he must wonder about the recovery rate among such individuals. How can they possibly be helped?

Little help or hope was offered to the rehabilitation of alcoholics until the organization of Alcoholics Anonymous was formed, at which time a powerful healing force was invoked to ease suffering. To see the gradual change that takes place on a mental level of an A.A. member is a thrilling example of mental healing, and such a happening may well be attributed to the strong force of love that gives A.A. its power to heal the obsessive personality.

It is not uncommon to hear a member behind the podium exclaim with great conviction: "I was *loved* back into Sobriety."

The healer can effectively help a person who is mentally disturbed by relying entirely on the power of his healing source to understand and communicate by mind with the sufferer. Techniques involving the use of the hands may be limited to, perhaps, just the head positions, while the consciousness of the healer stays in touch with Spirit. He will be guided as to what to say and do, and provided he keeps his mind stayed on his spirit source of power, very wonderfully effective results can be obtained.

Mental Healing Today

A growing number of hospital beds are being occupied in this country today by persons who have been diagnosed as having no clinical dysfunction, yet they are sick. In other words, there is some pressure that has pursued them until they have landed in the hospital with very real symptoms.

This century has witnessed the birth of a new interest and concern in easing disease related to mental pressure. Being a part of the effort through all its growing pains, the mental health field has made gigantic strides. With help from psychiatrists, psychologists, social workers, rehabilitation programs, community out-patient clinics, and similar sources, we do see our generation attacking the problems of society with new force.

Having been a student nurse at one time myself, I had the advantage of observing healing within the hospital setting. Certain opinions began to form in my mind on mental healing as a result of this experience.

As one enters a ward of persons who are suffering from mental pressures, one will almost without exception, find a close spiritual community, in a sense — composed of *patients only!* Somehow, an unspoken alliance exists among the patients with mutual concern one for the other. It seems as though the vulnerability of such persons has created a circle of defense to surround and wall out the mental pressures which made them ill in the first place.

A second observation envelops the belief that in many cases, chemotherapy is over-used in this country. Instead of having a person with a mental pressure, the situation is quickly converted into a *sedated* person with a mental pressure. At times when an individual is under great strain, the physician may feel justified in administering drugs; but from most cases I have seen, the person is handed a continued escape and is emphasizing a "deadening" of pain, rather than a solution of the problem which is causing the pain.

In this subtle avoidance of problem-solving which drug de-sensitizing permits, I have quite often heard patients admit to me that they have used this drug therapy consciously and subconsciously to "hide behind." I do not believe that anyone truly desires to carry a decapacitating load of mental burdens around with him. His problem is that he simply does not know how to use his spiritual power to get free of them.

It seems quite hopeful that in the future we may

anticipate more doctors, nurses, counselors, and anyone who desires to ease mental suffering to look to Spirit resources for more effective mental healing.

Of course, all of us probably know of people who are already doing this very thing. I shall never forget a dear doctor friend of mine who was treating me after I had experienced a severe emotional shock following a car accident.

From the moment I entered his office the first time, a healing began on a deep mental level. His patience, his deep spiritual love for me as his patient, and his sincere desire to see me well and happy again was very quickly sensed, and immediately I responded. This kind of healing which sprang from the spiritual nature of this devoted practitioner is what I attribute my healing to on that occasion.

Similar experiences must occur everyday between patient and healer. Any healing treatment based in love and compassion is the greatest service a practitioner can offer his Brother Man.

A Barrage of Symptoms

Not long ago, a middle-aged woman came to see Rev. Street for spiritual healing. She had every complaint in the book and then some, and as soon as a suggestion was offered to her for better health, she fired back with two negative aspects of the problem. Finally, he told her the truth about what he felt to be the real source of her difficulties.

Psychically, he had seen a certain disappointment with her husband some twenty years earlier which had caused great sorrow in her life, and as a result, she had bound and insulated herself with imaginary ills until a state of absolute misery was attained. If she really wanted to get well, it was going to be essential for her to face herself squarely and begin a "house cleaning."

With this direct approach to the problem, the woman began to weep and admitted that the healer was right. She had become totally absorbed in the "bad" state of her physical health, which was really a subconscious attempt to erase and cover the mental pressure of many years' weight.

Healing on the Spiritual Level

Having looked at mental disease as a problem of obsession, let us now approach spiritual disease as a result of possession. This distinction is very often misunderstood and should be emphasized in this particular approach to spiritual healing.

Here, "possession" is referring to the possession of a person by an entity.

As a child, a reference to an entity struck raw terror in my mind. I had heard horror stories from the pulpits of fundamental Christian churches, which always seemed to be directed toward someone's bad behavior. Within this frame of reference, I knew the story in the 8th chapter of Matthew's Gospel concerning the experience of Jesus' casting out devils from two persons who approached him. ". . . And he said unto them, Go. And when they were come out, they went into the herd of swine; and behold, the whole herd of swine ran violently down a steep place into the sea, and perished in the waters."

Needless to say, I did not feel too kindly toward devils or the like and was completely wrenched of any desire to establish any friendships with the ghouls about whom I had heard.

Therefore, my reaction for the next twenty years was to discount any tales which I heard on the matter of demons, attempting to hide the fear that was locked in my mind. For several years, I ascribed to the theory that there was no evil power in the world, only good — and this calculation afforded me great comfort.

It was not until I met Rev. Street several years ago that I felt I could trust anyone's source of information on the subject. Because of his training in New Zealand among the native tribes, and due to his extensive travels throughout the world, his experiences had added a depth of knowledge to his own personal beliefs in both white and black magic. As a result, I began to open my mind to his words and was met with much more satisfying answers than had been doled out to me in early childhood.

At best, I had become fairly well convinced that a possibility did exist in relation to the speculation of entity possession. However, there was a corner in my mind that still kicked at this belief. It was not until about two weeks ago that I "saw" for myself certain effects that were convincing.

While on this year's national tour, a woman made an appointment for spiritual healing. Her voice sounded rather casual as she explained that her problem was entity possession.

As I answered the door a few hours later, I met

a pretty young woman who stood smiling — a very dear soul seeking freedom.

Her story of how this thing had happened to her was relayed briefly; she had joined an organization which dealt with the development of psychic powers. Following a series of experiments in an attempt to communicate with her 'dead' husband, certain psychic centers were forced open prematurely. As a result, an entity had "hopped in." The woman was aware of what had happened and had sought help, but no one had been able to exorcise the entity. As she had practically given up hope, she came to Rev. Street with little conviction that any good could come from the visit.

Having worked with similar cases before, he immediately expected a tough time as the woman had been possessed for two years, and it was "locked" into place. Using a technique adopted from the Maoris, the healer began the attempt to help this lady. The blows which followed were described as the force of a baseball bat hitting her in the back. Her body shook as she literally hung onto the chair to stay in place.

At last, the ordeal was over, and she emerged from the room, a little shaken but feeling much better. The advice offered to her to prevent a repetition of this experience involved an effort to seek spiritual guidance through meditation and church attendance, as well as striving to lead a more spiritual life in every way.

She was only too happy to follow the instructions given to her, and she left that day with a new joy and gratitude for Rev. Street's assistance. I might

add that I came away with a new basis for belief
in entities.

Absent Healing

As St. Paul puts it, ''the fervent prayer of a right-
eous man will heal the sick,'' and all healing sanctu-
aries in the world possess many letters of the help
received in this manner, but it is stressed that this
practice is not the deepest method of absent healing.

The way of absent healing is a study in itself,
and its method is to make contact with the etheric
double of the patient concerned, which is done by the
''calling up'' of the etheric body and treating it in a
psychic manner. It is very difficult to impart this
knowledge to an aspiring healer who has not the
necessary experience, but Absent Healing can be
carried out by the healer's visualizing the person who
is sick and praying that the healing power will be
transmitted to the sufferer.

With some practice, it is possible for the healer
to develop the ability to see the spirit body of the
sufferer and to convey therapeutic forces to the person
concerned. He need not know the person; the etheric
body will be shown to him, as invariably Spirit comes
to mind rather than mind going to Spirit. Very effective Absent Healing treatment can be given which
takes root in the consciousness of the patient via the
subconscious mind. However, it is stressed that this
technique cannot be learned quickly but comes only
with practice and identification with psychic healing
in a total sense.

It is important in the early stages that the healer

does not "take on" the condition of the patient into
his own physical body. This happening occurs frequently, because too much of the healer's mind enters
into the picture and not enough separation between
mind and spirit. The healer, after all, is using psychic power only to make contact with the spiritual
side of the sufferer. Thus activated, the spirit will re-
establish health in the diseased area, and it is frequent
for healers to assume the patient's sickness in a type
of reflex action process. It is important that a stop be
put on this occurrence immediately; otherwise, the
healer is likely to suffer dreadfully as a result of the
manifold sicknesses coming back to take root in his
own make-up. If he cares to make a cross with his
mind over the patient who is either sitting or lying
down, and allows the flow of his Christ love to contact
the spirit of the sufferer, he will afford a separation
so that no influence can come from the patient's
malady.

It is also vital that he be protected psychically,
because this is an area where the spirit forces who
are mischievous or possessive will try to contact him.
Therefore, prior to the healing session, it is well for
the healer to pray for protection, power, and love to
surround him and to be channeled through him to
the sufferer.

The healer will take great care that his body is
scrupulously clean, and if he smokes, that he does
not do so prior to the healing session. The wearing
of a white coat is both protective and hygienic. Not
only does it look nice, but it feels good and gives the
patient a confidence in the healer, which is vital. Thus,
clothed in humility and great compassion for the pa-

tient, the healer is ready for any developments, for he is attuned to his Father in heaven and also to his brother or sister who is suffering in some way.

Rev. Street was the first healer I had known who used Absent Healing in his work. The process he uses requires a snapshot of the person and a brief history of the physical anomalies. In hearing of this area of his ministry, I sent him a picture of my father who was suffering agony from rheumatoid arthritis. Having been active all his life, he suddenly found the onset of this problem to be immobilizing so that he was forced to stay in bed.

At the time, Rev. Street was 1500 miles away, and we wondered if the distance would really make a difference in the effectiveness of the treatment. To our great joy, the pain was completely gone after only three days, and immediately he was out of bed and back to his daily routine of fishing!

Such occurrences, I found later, are common in the life of the healer. Everyday many letters arrive on his doorstep relating the joy of healing that has been channeled through his unselfish service into the lives of his Brother Man.

Healing During Sleep

An unusual healing practice can be experienced during sleep provided the sleeper is well-grounded in the requirements which must be adhered to beforehand. In a certain manner the dreamer implants the seed of healing before going to sleep, and if a layer of subconscious hope is not the motive in seeking self-healing, then there is a good chance that the healing process will develop during the night. Of course, this matter is a complete study in itself *

The Paute Indians seem to have known of this healing power long ago when one spoke: "Whenever I dream, I talk to something in the darkness. I talk to my power. That is why I have lived so long.. . ."

---

* See Noel Street's book, DREAMER AWAKE!, for further details on dream experience. This book can be ordered from The Lotus Ashram, 128 NE 82 Terrace, Miami, Florida 33138. $3.00 postpaid.

Chapter 18

The Human Aura

The development of the aura can be vitally important in relation to healing, and every individual has a choice in this aspect of his own development.

In giving many lectures on the aura, Rev. Street adds valuable details and explanations which are not readily found in most books on the subject.

First of all, what is the aura? In simple terms, it is the magnetic field of vibration which surrounds every person in the same way a light emanates from a candle or a flower. Clairvoyantly, the glow appears as a mass of color which varies in size, area, and formation with each individual. In fact, the accuracy in the aura can be reliable so as to identify fully one's habits, thoughts, diseases, and potential, as well as his current understanding and state of spiritual development.

Artists With Color Scopes

Even as the eyes are said to be the mirror of the Soul, so too does the aura reflect the light of an aspirant's spiritual consciousness. It is altered and developed in accordance with the will of the person, as well as his conscious and subconscious ability to identify with the spiritual life. Hence, one has no dif-

193

ficulty in understanding why the auras of saints, sages, and gurus are depicted as shining lights.

Sometimes called the auric envelope, this light is protective against the forces of darkness as well as having the purpose of acting as a field of absorption for spiritual conveyances, direction, and power. So now let us view ourselves as the artists possessing the color scope of God, setting out to paint our own auric pattern.

Development During Pregnancy And After Birth

Another name for the aura is 'garment of the soul.' As a result of pregnancy, the size of the mother's aura increases, and the astral body of the embryo is attached at the solar plexus where knowledge of past karma and earlier earth lives is stored. At birth, a small white glow known as the etheric sheath or astral envelope appears around the child.

The purpose and function of the aura is to surround the seven bodies which accompany the incoming spirit — the physical, mental, emotional, and etheric bodies, connecting with the bodies of the Father, the Son, and the Holy Spirit, sometimes referred to as our "Higher Triad."

The shape of the body to be born is decided by the etheric mold. The creation of this mold has been produced by the influence of sound vibrations emitted from the zygote — the permanent atom or individual essence to which all past history is attached.

Each zygote has a distinctive sound or musical note, and all growth throughout the life of the individual vibrates to that particular hum. Some people know their own note even while they are alive, and the purpose of the sounding of the ''AUM'' in the previous chapter on meditation is to stabilize and draw upward to the consciousness of the meditator that vibratory link which leads to his spiritual self. As Rev. Street has so beautifully said: ''By learning your own wave-length, you find your own 'Father-Soul.'''

It is interesting to note that New Zealand's Maori people know when the time of their death is approaching, as they hear their own vibratory sound clearly, and thus, are able to prepare for the forthcoming transition.

A Characteristic Perfume

Each person is further individualized by a characteristic smell. It was fascinating to hear a report from Rev. Street's younger daughter, Olivia, who recently had the privilege of visiting a certain tribe in the Pacific. Upon approaching a grandmother in the tribe who was nearly blind, the old woman spent a long time ''smelling'' or familiarizing herself with the young girl's perfume, so that there would be no mistaken identity on a future visit.

The Fijian people are similarly sensitive in this way and can discern the presence of certain spirits in the room. Oftentimes, Rev. Street has heard a Fijian exclaim, ''My father is here; I can sense him!'' And this awareness is through smell. However, this ability is really not unusual, for Saint Paul establishes the discernment of spirits as an available gift to us all, should we wish to develop it.

The Power of the Aura

Many auric changes occur during an individual's lifetime, which are related mainly to potency as the Light enters and reconstructs the consciousness into a closer association with its Divine Self.

Some years ago, the great Indian Master, Sri Ramana Maharshi, was on his death bed, and his physical body was suffering intense pain. In order to placate a disciple, he agreed to have a physician come in, although he was aware that the time had come for his transition into Higher Life. The busy physician hurried into the room with bag in hand, anxious to get on to the next call and very quickly approached the bed of the small, wrinkled-faced man. Suddenly, without warning, he could get no closer and stopped in his tracks, some eight feet from the bed. Sinking to his knees, the doctor was unable to move. He had, in fact, entered the auric range of this beloved guru and was unaccustomed to the resulting high vibrations of light.

Quickly sensing the situation, Maharshi spoke kindly to him and encouraged him to approach the bed and carry on with the task at hand. In the doctor's own words, his life was changed from that moment, transforming him into a devotee of this great Indian teacher.

To summarize then: (1) The aura is a part of us, even as the perfume is to a flower; (2) the aura is protective and formative; (3) it provides a permanent record for our history; and (4) this manifestation is our link with God, which can alter as our evolution proceeds.

The Relationship to Karma

Recently, Rev. Street made quite a surprising comment which was a completely new thought for me and merited a good deal of attention. It concerned the relationship of the aura to an individual's karma.

"The aura of the individual is *decided* by his karma," he said. Explaining further, the healer correlated the prevalence of either the base, physical colors or the higher spiritual ones with the effort an individual is initiating in overcoming those conditions relating to his past history.

Should the lower colors of red, orange, or yellow be vibrating more frequently in his aura, it is a sign that he is living more in the physical and mental levels.

As the color green appears therein, it represents the neutralizing force in the color pattern, having a balancing effect between the physical and spiritual planes.

And finally, as the pale blue, indigo, and violet begin to show themselves, they portray the light of an aspirant who is effectively using his spiritual power to overcome his own karmic conditions.

Thus, those individuals whose auric make-up predominantly displays the higher vibrations of the blues and violet are definitely accomplishing those things for which they have reincarnated, in a spiritual sense.

Of course, the auric pattern of colors can be altered from lower to higher vibrations as the individual desires and directs the use of his own spiritual will to a greater degree.

How Can It Change

We must remember that the aura and its components penetrate and interpenetrate the physical body. Therefore, even as thoughts are things, and our countenance expresses to some degree our thought nature, so too, are the various colors in our aura conditioned by our activities and the manner in which we expend the energy of our nature.

The average aura radiates about two feet beyond the human body, and the various colors have these meanings:

RED: the person who is, at the moment, thinking very physically.

ORANGE: a person engaged in commerce, business, finance, or the mundane processes of our work-a-day world.

YELLOW: an intellectual person making use of his mind.

GREEN: a loving person who is not too tied down by either the mind or material activities; at the same time, green is a color that does not reflect one's highest spiritual nature. It is really an in-between color.

BLUE: Pale blue — represents generosity.

         Dark blue — person is a devotee of spiritual matters, thought, activity.

VIOLET: spirituality

GOLD: sometimes seen around a person's aura reflects their spiritual development.

MOTHER OF PEARL: a color very rarely seen in individuals other than saints or persons in a state of illumination.

A Child's Aura

As the individuality of the child commences to unfold, so then does the aura develop. Some readers may have seen the beautiful paintings of the Christ Child depicted with all the lovely colors of the spectrum surrounding Him in a perfect blending — yet pale, as His ministry had not become active to any degree. But in an ordinary life, the color of the aura quickly changes along with the varying moods.

Since we are the aura builders by our own will, we can purposefully direct our lives and follow a pathway which is spiritually active. Likewise, the beauty of our inner Light will reflect in our eyes, on our countenance, in our voice, and through our aura.

The Eight-Fold Pathway

Looking at the teachings of the Gautama Buddha who lived 600 B.C., one sees the ease with which his instructions could be applied today. His eight-fold path was a guide to followers who wished to find illumination, and it was a way which he had diligently sought for himself. When Gautama knew that he had found it, he began to teach it to others:

> Right thought
> Right speech
> Right actions
> Right food
> Right means of livelihood
> Right beliefs
> Right faith
> Right meditation

Alternatively, we can poison our auras by reversing

these principles. We walk, talk, and live in the aura of our own creation. We may choose to be on-color or off-color, according to our wishes.

I have often heard Rev. Street tell the story of his mother who really understood very little about auras, except that they do exist. On a certain day, she returned to her house after being away for awhile. Knowing that a certain woman had been in whom she did not like, she exclaimed fervently: "That awful woman, coming to our house again and dragging her dirty aura all over the place!"

There was a lovely woman in Wellington, New Zealand, who had experienced a most difficult time in her marriage and had persevered with great patience. Later, Noel asked her to name three important qualities in marriage which she believed would help people who were having difficulty in this area. What had she herself found to be most helpful? A few days later after thinking it over, she replied that there was only one quality which mattered, as far as she was concerned, and that was kindness. To reinforce that conviction, that woman's face and aura shone with such brightness all the time, that if she were standing out in the street collecting for some cause, she would invariably come away with three or four times as much as anyone else.

So the painting of the aura is in our hands. This effort can be associated with our character and ability to live in a calm, purposeful way. When the aura is strong, we will feel a more focused alignment with the physical, and spiritual powers return with soul memories. Indeed, we can join with the Master in saying: "I and my Father are One."

Chapter 19

Techniques from Other Healers

White man is well-known for his prejudices which force him to believe that his own healing techniques are the only really acceptable methods in our modern world. It is interesting to notice that our minds, however, are opening from the suppressed or orthodox viewpoint to a broader concept. Consequently, many so-called primitive remedies are being used in healing today. An example is *curare,* which was originally used in South America to stun or anesthetize the victims of hunters. We read also of witch doctors in South Africa who conduct classes to share their knowledge, either inherited or attained through psychic attunement.

One of the paradoxes of human suffering is that wherein we are flexible and free-thinking in most areas of life, our physical bodies are treated with a standard which is quite contrary and closed to new ideas. Conditioned thinking probably applies more in relation to medical science than to anything else in our society.

The Era of New Thought

Because of the upheaval in religious thought, we have pulled the lids off some age-old myths and enjoy a new degree of spiritual enlightenment. To a lesser

201

extent, the same freedom has come into our political and national economy. Similarly, the freedom of new ideas is noticed in war and peace, family life, love, education, entertainment, and a deep reverential respect for life in all forms.

The kind of dress we choose with which to clothe ourselves may be unusual and something out of the ordinary, yet as soon as that body becomes unhealthy, we are caught in the same old patterns of orthodoxy in relation to health and healing. With all the prejudices and legal complications, we can well ask ourselves, "Who is freer — the civilized man living in an ultra-modern society, or a primitive staked out in the jungle?"

A Return to the Village

Last year, Noel met a Jewish husband in New Mexico whose wife was a Navajo Indian. Having several children and a very happy marriage, the gentleman explained his wife's technique when she or the children were ill.

"Whenever any of them need medical attention, my wife returns to her old tribe and seeks the help of the medicine man. She returns only when they are cured."

Intrigued with this story, Noel asked further, "Do you ever accompany her?"

"No," was the reply. "I don't really have much understanding of their practices, but she always comes back well, and that's what is important to me."

Seeing these occasional glimpses into the natural healing remedies which are around us is most inter-

esting if we are sufficiently wise thinking. Here, again
in relation to any form of spiritual or psychic healing, the old adage applies that "when the pupil is
ready, the knowledge will be made available to
him."

On his last visit to Ohio, Noel was pleased to meet
a Cherokee woman who was serving as a maid in
one of the large hotels. Finding that he had an interest in her beliefs and background, she commented:

"We pass our knowledge down by word of mouth.
When I am ready for more, I get called back to the
hills to my people."

What a privilege it is to hear these stories of the
Indian people. Some readers may have had the opportunity of seeing an Indian healer, although no
such one would 'advertize' his powers. However, if
the spectator should indicate his willingness to learn —
instead of seeking to gain something for himself —
then he would be more ready to share this experience.
From another viewpoint, if an 'outsider' were sick
and genuinely sought help from a medicine man in
any part of the world, the healer would be pleased
to use his skill in an effort to bring an easement to
suffering.

Approaching Indian Lore

Very often, photographing, writing about, or sell-
ing is the closest many people come to true Indian
lore. For instance, a sand painting is as remote to
most of us as the thoughts of a crocodile, yet the
Indian healer creates this form with delicacy and effort
in an attempt to make another's life better. To him,

he is invoking the Ageless Spirit of Healing through his painting of an intricate design. At the end of each day, the multi-colored picture is erased so that a new one can be established the following day.

Today there are still many Indian healers who possess strong psychic powers. On reservations and in certain areas of this country, the sacred houses or kivas exist which are used for healing ceremonies as well as for worship and communication.

Maori "Houses of Wisdom"

These kivas correspond almost identically to the wharekuras of the Maori people in New Zealand. Termed "houses of wisdom," they serve as the abodes of priests, trainee healers, and persons whose lives are dedicated to service of their Brother Man. Frequently, the wharekuras remain in absolute darkness, and a person entering therein can quickly sense the great reverence in the atmosphere.

Herbal Cure for Cancer

Maori healing practices consist of many herbal remedies which have been passed on by word of mouth down the centuries. Rev. Street has watched an old Maori woman preparing a life-saving blend of herbs which was known to cure cancer. She would send children out into the forests to fetch a particular herb. Telling each child where to go to find what she wanted, none of them knew how many herbs were utilized in the mixture or what they actually were. However, it is known that the remedy did contain an herb known as "tuti," which is such a strong poison that it killed an elephant a few years ago in New Zealand that happened to graze upon the plant in its wild state. To see this same herb benefit human beings when taken in the right quantity tells the story of skillful folk medicine.

Healing Chants

The tohungas or Maori occult priests make frequent use of their spiritual power through chants called kairakias. They have also been passed down by word of mouth, and the healing qualities therein are directly attributed to the active sound vibration which can change matter. The kairakias can be tremendously valuable in a large country such as New Zealand, with a population of only 2 ½ million people. In some isolated areas, a trip to a physician could mean an all-day journey, and to be able, for example, to remove a fish bone immediately from a child's throat by a form of psychic healing is a wonderful quality. Once, Rev. Street asked such a healer if he ever had an opportunity to go to church, and he replied, "No, no, I don't. But I talk to my Mate up there everyday, all the time."

The use of fresh water is a must with Maori healers, both as a remedy and as a purifying agent. In fact, one healer transports a tub of sea water daily for use by his patients, as he prefers to have each one fully submerged prior to treatment. Likewise, all healers everywhere agree on this necessity to be scrupulously clean.

The Philippine Psychic Healers

A certain method of psychic surgery used in the Philippines is an astonishing sight. Many people who have had this method of treatment applied personally can testify to the effectiveness of these psychic operations where the flesh is opened by the bare hands of the healers. There appear to be about twenty of these surgeons who are actively practising — notably, Brother Terte, Tony Agpaoa, Gonzales, Ahding, and Camelo.

The British Isles and England

The British Isles have long been renowned for their interest in psychic healing, and thousands of healers practice today in various parts of this ancient place. Such practitioners may even appear as a band of roving gypsies who call at one's doorstep to sell items such as clothes pins, tell fortunes, cure your warts and worries, help your love life, and so on. The effectiveness of some of these people's cures is surprising.

"The King's Touch" was originally developed in England in medieval times. It was the custom for the sick to visit the king to receive his touch, and many people are reported to have been healed in consequence. However, the kings themselves abused the power which the prayers of their loyal subjects had developed for them in a psychic sense. Thus, the followers eventually lost confidence in their power to heal and the practice disappeared. It is quite interesting to know that psychic healers are allowed to treat patients in many British hospitals.

Generally, healing is carried out by the laying on of hands and the use of psychic power to produce a change in the patient. The healing work of Jess Thomas in England which was mentioned earlier, on the other hand, was an exceptional method and gift. This man was well-known through many public appearances in town halls and on television.

Many evidences of healing followed Jess' physical death, but one of the most remarkable experiences occurred in Melbourne.

Attending the Spiritualist Church one Sunday morning, an invitation had been extended for Rev. Street to speak at one of the following week-day services. As the healer sat quietly in meditation that morning in the beautiful old church, he saw Jess' light psychically and began to communicate with his friend.

"Why don't you do a psychic healing demonstration on Sunday and let me work through you?" queried Jess.

"I'd like to," returned Noel, "but they haven't asked me."

"Well, we're working on the President of the Church right now."

On hearing this suggestion, Noel opened his eyes to peer at the figure sitting on the platform near the front of the hall. The man sat still and seemed to be half-asleep, no discernible expression on his face.

When the meeting was over, the President directly approached Noel and asked with unexpected enthusiasm, "Would you be able to speak at the Sunday service next week?"

"Yes. Would you care to see a psychic healing

demonstration with Jess Thomas working through
me?''

As Mr. George Eldred, the President, was familiar
with the psychic surgery carried out by Jess Thomas,
the idea was most favorably accepted, so that the
following Sunday morning found the place packed to
capacity with eager on-lookers.

The ''operating table'' was, in reality, an old
massage couch covered with a sheet, and the first
patient to approach the platform was a woman with
an eye weakness.

As the healer stood before the prone figure, he
felt his body stiffen as Jess entered it. Fully aware of
his surroundings Rev. Street heard the woman de-
tailing her eye complaint, so he placed his hands over
that particular area of the body. At once, however,
he heard Jess' voice emphasizing:

''Put your hands on her legs!''

Quite bewildered, he then heard himself repeating
Jess' words to the patient: ''How are your legs
now?''

''You should know, Mr. Thomas,'' she
laughed.

''How are your feet?'' he continued.

''Just fine, Mr. Thomas,'' she laughed again.

As the intermediary 'surgeon,' Rev. Street could
not understand the meaning of this strange conver-
sation, since she had come specifically for eye treatment, so finally he dismissed it from his mind.

When the meeting drew to a close with all the patients treated, the President was thanking Noel for his
healing demonstration when the first lady stood up
in the middle of the congregation. She explained that

Mr. Thomas had treated her in England five years earlier when he was alive. In fact, she had traveled all the way from Australia to Brighton, England, so that he could treat a leg and foot ailment. Apparently, she and Jess had "taken up" where their patient-healer relationship had left off — an extraordinary experience which Noel Street had never anticipated.

The United States

Many fine healers in this country have produced wonderfully effective results, either by public demonstrations or quiet services in homes and churches. To have an opportunity to witness Kathryn Kuhlman in one of her public healing meetings is, indeed, a real pleasure. At all meetings, people respond to the marvelous Power which is invoked by this fine servant. Her book, *I Believe in Miracles,* is an inspiration to all readers.

Another great channel for healing is Agnes Sanford. Her quiet, dignified, and modest presentation, both verbally and in her books, is a fine example of humility backed by a strong healing power.

Public attention is quickly being drawn to the most effective work of Willard Fuller whose gift seems to lie in the specialty of healing teeth. On one occasion, Rev. Street asked Mr. Fuller if he knew the source of his help, and he replied that it was of a divine nature — although he did not believe that it was specifically from a Guide or one spirit source. What is not so well-known about this type of healing, perhaps, is that several people in different parts of the world received this dental healing gift about the same time. Mr. Fuller said he knew of six persons who are similarly blessed.

Disease and Karma

With so many different healing techniques in the world, one might wonder which is the most effective? Healers are sometimes more able to help with certain patients than with others. Furthermore, a healer may be quite able to bring healing readily to a specific ailment. So the question is not really, "Can a person be healed?" but rather, "What is the karma relating to the disease?"

Rev. Street once explained to me that he never refused to treat a patient who asked for help. My most acute question followed: "Well, what about the little Mongoloid child with chromosome defects?"

He said that he had treated such a child, but ". . . at times a soul's karmic bank is too full," so that no apparent response occurs. Sometimes, however, the parents' karma is also deeply involved as to how they relate to their children, normal or abnormal.

On the other hand, if a patient's health can be restored, and the karmic pattern lifted from the situation, then it matters very little who the healer is or what method he uses.

Healing, Past and Present

Whatever techniques we may employ today in an effort to develop healing power has almost certainly been used in the past. Some of the old embalmed bodies from Egypt dating back 4,000 years have revealed skulls which have been partly removed surgically and a brain operation carried out.

Going back still further to the city of Ur on the mouth of the Euphrates River, we find that many women physicians practiced medicine some 5,000 years ago. So disease and its healing have always been one of the most mysterious of all enigmas.

Broadly speaking, healing has forever fallen into two distinct categories: the orthodox and the unorthodox. Perhaps before the covers finally wither off the last copy of this book, we may find that in keeping with a trend towards a universal language, a universal monetary system, and universal law, so too, a universal approach to the healing art may also arise. As Rev. Street tends to believe, this new thought on sickness will relate far more to prevention, arrived at through unified study and a greater understanding of the law of the cause, i.e., karma.

Developing As A Healer

Should you ever feel in any way influenced to develop as a healer yourself, it is helpful to remember that there are many persons in need of treatment. As you become qualified to heal, some will be directed to you for the easement of their suffering.

You may prefer a certain technique which has been referred to here. Or, you may well find that it is best not to follow anyone, but to be guided solely by Spirit in your development. At first, healers tend to apply various techniques until they find the ones which best work for them. Invariably, the effective ways relate more to the use of psychic power or the ability to tune in to a greater healing power in Spirit than to the use of herbs or outside remedies.

Some healers find that they never touch a patient physically. For the most part, healing is done through the mind or through the spirit; either process is ultimately based in compassion for the sick. Of course, it is prudent to wait until asked to treat an illness or to help a person in a physical sense. But there is nothing to prevent one from directing his prayers and mental power to the patient.

So whatever methods you should develop, be very sure that the Spirit of Healing will accompany you on the Pathway, bringing joy to the healer and the healed.

Chapter 20

Observations of the Street Ministry

Since I first became associated with Noel Street, I have heard, read numerous letters, and actually seen for myself the results of his unusual ministry. Suddenly, healing was no longer a theory of words or a long-lost hope of desperate people — it became the live, vibrant power of the spiritual world bringing evidential change into physical matter.

The first case that I ever heard of who had received healing help directly from him was a friend named Marlene in Texas who was a vivacious grandmother in her 50's. Without any warning one day, she had become violently ill with symptoms resembling some cardiac dysfunction and was rushed to the hospital for emergency treatment. After numerous painstaking tests, the laboratory report was not at all conclusive as to the source of the difficulty. Thus, she was released from the hospital with a load of doubts in her mind.

Within several weeks another attack occurred, and back she went to the hospital. This time the tests revealed some vague chemical imbalance which was treated rather ineffectually.

When Noel Street arrived in her area on a tour, Marlene made haste to see him about the symptoms she was still experiencing. Using his psychic faculties, the healer very quickly "saw" the emotional pressures which had brought on the physical symptoms. Able to see the reasons herself in a new light, she began to make a tremendous effort to relieve the adverse environmental pressures around her.

Included in Rev. Street's treatment were several beneficial Yoga postures along with necessary changes in her diet. Ten months later, we saw Marlene again, and she was glowing! Her whole appearance spoke for her excellent state of health. To add to her happiness, she offered, "I plan to start teaching Yoga in a few more months, and I'm so excited about life!"

Attitudes Toward Healing

Of course, many different attitudes exist about healing. It is not uncommon for a family member to be torn in loyalty over his own convictions and those of a spouse, for instance.

A few months ago, a young mother brought her son, David, for treatment. The child suffered with a grave bronchial problem. The woman admitted that her husband was quite opposed to spiritual healing, feeling that it lacked the necessary sophistication of the medical profession.

After Rev. Street checked the boy, he recommended a chest expander. Hearing this suggestion, the father was firm to point out that the expander might build up the muscles of the chest but would have no positive effect on the condition. However, David greatly anticipated this new "toy," and his enthusiasm finally won him the equipment.

The mother continued to bring him for healing treatment, and within three weeks the child was practically 100% improved. So noticed a friend who commented to the father on the child's rapid recovery.

"Oh, yes," came the reply, "We've been taking him to a new *doctor,* who recommended a chest expander."

Upon hearing the story later, Rev. Street laughed. "Well, do thank him for the confidence. That's the fastest anyone has ever gotten a medical degree!"

"Black Swallows"

It is not uncommon for patients to come asking for healing of some minor nature, when actually they are hiding a more severe difficulty in their lives. There are many incidents in Noel Street's history wherein Spirit has revealed numerous "hidden" problems in order to ease suffering.

Such was the case of a woman who came in with a shoulder complaint. While the healer was treating her, he was shown a psychic picture of a flock of birds swooping over her; being a bird lover himself, he had no difficulty in identifying them as black swallows.

Attempting to interpret this scene from his mind's eye, he asked if she had any birds where she was living.

"No," came the reply.

"Well, do you feel an affinity towards black swallows?"

"No," again.

Then suddenly the meaning struck him! "Are you drinking something that isn't good for you?"

Immediately, the woman became irritated and cried out, "I know it . . . I know I shouldn't have come! I told my friend that you would find out!"

Wondering what this outburst meant, the truth was finally arrived at through her sobs. Because of a sorrow in her domestic life, she had been drinking a fifth of liquor a day in an effort to block out the emotional pain. Getting down to the real issue, the healer was able to help her with the various problems which she felt were too overwhelming to face.

A Patient From Boston

As a healer, one experiences a steady stream of patients who seek help at all hours of the day or night, exhibiting a wide range of ills. Many patients will travel many miles to receive treatment.

Not long ago, the Ashram telephone rang, and a man named Ben was at the other end of the line. He asked if he could come to Miami for a week to receive healing for a severe case of arthritis. His confidence in Rev. Street's work was sparked by the fine response his wife had made a year earlier when she had sought treatment in Boston.

Arrangements were made, and the couple were soon on their way. Upon arriving, a healing schedule was drawn up so that Ben could come in for treatment at regular intervals. Rev. Street, on the first session, found that the arthritis had spread throughout the arms and legs, making movement of the extremities most difficult.

However, on the second morning, Ben came in all smiles. To everyone's delight he was stretching his arms above his head! By the end of the week such a change had occurred that he was able to return to Boston, completely free of the pain-killing drugs which he had needed for the discomfort, and he was much improved in every way.

To express their gratitude, the couple wrote out a substantial check to cover the installation of an air-conditioner in the healing Sanctuary.

A letter followed telling of Ben's continued improvement. Such experiences add much light and happiness to the life of a healer.

White and Black Magic

One thing which makes the Street ministry so unique is a vast knowledge of black magic. Having learned much in a setting which the New Zealand "Bush" provides, his healing experience in relation to black magic has benefited more people than one would suspect.

This subject of the light and dark forces has fascinated me, and a question is never far away when we begin to discuss it. One thing Noel explained to me was that "light has power, darkness has power." This phrase is translated from the Maori language, and the significant factor between the two is motive. Some individuals are quite willing to work for the dark forces if some personal gain can be attained, whether it be power, wealth, or some special favors.

A certain woman in Sydney was being controlled

by a black magician. In her decision to work in black magic, she herself had killed two people. However, she finally decided that she no longer wished to be a part of this kind of practice. Knowing of her decision, the magician began to direct his strength in an effort to kill her.

When the young woman arrived at Rev. Street's apartment with her boyfriend, it was evident from the pale face that she was quite ill. It was explained that her death was destined to come the next day, on Black Friday.

Through the long night that followed, a struggle ensued between the forces of light and darkness. Just as the magician was using his power adversely, the healer used his power to counteract the evil force.

As the morning light dawned, the color returned to the girl's cheeks, and a prayer of gratitude was offered. Without any question, a repentant soul had been welcomed back into Light, even as spiritual healing had overcome darkness in the world through this servant of Mankind.

The Crystal Gazer

Should one have an opportunity to follow this healer around for a few days, he would probably be most impressed by the numerous evidences of Spirit's closeness at all times, made manifest through psychic powers.

One of the most remarkable incidents of his ministry could be told of a certain crystal gazer he met unexpectedly one day.

Some friends had telephoned him one morning and invited him to leave London with them and journey to the seacoast town of Brighton for a visit. Quite happy to get away from the city, he agreed to go and soon found himself sitting on a bench overlooking the sea.

Very shortly, a little girl came up to him and began to talk, and then the child's mother appeared.

How old is she?'' the healer asked.

"Three years," came the reply.

"She's really very old, isn't she?''

With this unusual question, the mother gave a start and then laughed, understanding the depth behind the comment.

Because Rev. Street had recognized the degree of this woman's spiritual awareness, he continued: "And what are you doing with your gift?''

"I am a crystal gazer. My name is Madame Georgette."

Somewhat surprised, the healer asked her if she was working on that particular day.

"Yes, if you'd like." So they went to her tiny cubical where readings were given.

Instructing Rev. Street in the use of the crystal ball, the reader then took the object from him and began to spin off several details which seemed fairly inconsequential. But soon her face began to whiten and grow serious as she fixed her eyes on some point within the ball.

"I see you in a long white coat. You are standing in a hall talking to some people. You are a healer!'' Her voice reflected a heightened degree of interest, verging on astonishment.

When the fact of his ministry as healer was con-
firmed, the meaning of the reader's amazement was
disclosed.

"I've been praying for you to come!" she volun-
teered, obviously excited. "Just this morning I was in
the Cathedral lighting candles and praying that a
healer would be sent to me!"

Soon this woman's incredible story had been
poured out. Because this crystal gazer did have certain
psychic powers, she knew that a one-time associate
was attempting to kill her little girl through psychic
means. She had actually seen him appearing to the
child on the astral level as a snake, his identity being
recognized through the eyes.

Each time he appeared, the child was terrified and
would scream, "Mommy, that horrible snake is back
again!"

As this occurrence became more frequent, the
mother was understandably grieved, as she did not
know how to protect the child. Thus, each day the
visit to the Cathedral was of utmost urgency, as she
prayed for help.

Fortunately, the healer was quite able to deal with
this problem, and quickly the dark force was erad-
icated.

In the years that followed, Madame Georgette and
Rev. Street's family remained close friends.

To me, this one story is indicative of the marvelous
Spirit of Light which is ever close to the lives of those
individuals who would seek it. In a beautiful way it
was channeled to a child in need.

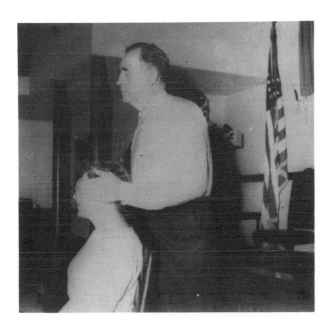

Rev. Street Healing in Long Beach, California

Chapter 21

Combating Pressure Through Harmony

With so much pressure in today's world, it is *you* who must take the initiative in insulating yourself, if there is to be any hope of happiness and good health. Without a doubt, an attempt to change the world would be futile, but changing *ourselves* is a much more likely prospect and a full-time job. Provided one is willing to make the effort to do certain, simple things — as well as establish right principles — he will inevitably build a harmonious way of life for himself and those persons around him.

To keep disease-free and promote a state of harmony, Rev. Street often makes certain suggestions to his patients which are equally applicable here.

1. *Keep a Pet*

For all animal-lovers, the keeping of a pet can be an invaluable way of meeting tension. Consider the elderly lady in a large city who is perhaps widowed. For her to be alone all day without friends or visitors, she could become extremely frustrated and unhappy. But to have a pet, let us say a bird, to talk to and feed each day, would make a tremendous difference in her life.

If the animal were a dog or a cat, think of the increased joy and pleasure such companionship would offer. There is an aged woman in our neighborhood

who can be spotted at regular intervals each day,
walking her beloved dog around the block. To look
at them, a strange resemblance exists, so that any
passerby would readily know that these two friends
belong together.

Children always find happiness in owning an animal. In fact, such an experience seems to be an in-
separable part of childhood. And to see an individual
who has brought with him into adulthood the same
ability to extend a free flow of love to the lesser
creatures is a marvelous experience.

Recently, I heard the story of a young fellow who
had gone to Rev. Street for an Akashic Reading. His
story seemed to unfold bearing the truth of how he
had learned to love.

It seems that all through his life, he had been
lonely and felt quite unable to uncover from within
the capacity to express affection or love. After 35
years of this isolation, a neighbor died and left a
little furry dog who needed a new master. Because
no one around wanted the animal, the man agreed
to keep it until another home could be found.

After several weeks of caring for the pup, an unspoken allegiance somehow developed between the
two loners, and the dog became so attached to his
new friend that he readily became the watchdog and
guardian around the place. He strongly challenged
anyone with sharp, threatening barks, who came
near his newfound master, and consequently, the
young chap began to respond to this loyalty with
a strange new emotion for him — love.

As the visitor explained to the healer, it was this
form of love coming from a small, seemingly in-

significant creature, that induced the most marvelous experience of his life!

2. *Enjoy Music*

The power of music is a balm to the soul of man. One need not necessarily be a musician to anchor himself in the calm of this great luxury. To lose oneself in the blend of countless vibrations of sound is a giant step in the direction of right living through harmony.

A certain young soldier suffered severe emotional shock during World War II. After being sent to a Veteran's Hospital for several months, his condition seemed to deteriorate in that he fell further into the depths of unresponsiveness. Finally, a music therapist spotted the patient on the ward and asked that he be brought to the music room for the next session.

The physician doubted that this kind of therapy could benefit the young man who sat in a trance-like state day in and day out, but he agreed to release him to the therapist's charge for lack of any better solutions of his own.

After a week, the musician observed that the patient invariably responded to the rich sound of the violin, so she began to spend additional time each day playing this instrument for him. Patiently she waited for any encouraging responses which might subtly appear, and at last the day came when he spoke a few words to her. With gradual improvement, the young soldier was permitted more and more free time each day in the music room.

At last, the moment came when the patient walked into the room and raised the violin to his chin with soft grace. As he touched the bow to the strings, a lovely melody of long ago floated through a room that was strangely hushed. The beauty of his expression utterly amazed the therapist and the other patients! No one had suspected that he had played the violin before the war, and it was this return to tranquility and wholeness, through music, that offered him another opportunity to walk among his fellows once more with renewed health and strength. Indeed, such gifts must be from a Father who created Man's delicate ear for beauty.

Throughout the busy day, music can be a balancing factor for any of us who seek harmony in our lives. Oftentimes when I have become downhearted with some really unimportant incident, I quickly switch on a record or the radio, and am almost instantly at one with life again, simply by the power which music exerts over my being.

And not only is music able to mold our waking hours, but also quite capable of tuning in our ears to the inner spirit world. Should you care to play some kind of pleasing melody ten or fifteen minutes before retiring at night, you would be cushioning your dream bed with new softness as you prepare to enter the other world of heightened consciousness.

3. *Walk Frequently*

To plan an ''outing'' each day is a sure way to combat tension. Whether one walks slowly or fast, he will soon establish his own pace which will be most relaxing to the body and mind. For those persons who get limited exercise, scheduling a daily walk is essential for good health.

A car which is not run a little every day soon becomes sluggish and eventually will not run at all. Our bodies, likewise, need the necessary stimulation to remain in an excellent working condition.

Last year, a dear friend was going through a divorce after 25 years of marriage. Instead of seeing all the negative aspects of the situation (and there were quite a few!), she began to work on her own thinking and completely reversed the whole course of the unexpected upheaval in her life. One thing she did each day and night was to go for a long walk, breathing deeply and concentrating on relaxation of body and mind. It was her belief later, that this simple routine did more for her outlook than anything else in staying on top of the circumstances.

4. *Practice Yoga*

As a continuation of the effort to relieve tension, Yoga is an excellent way to bring ease into the body, mind, and spirit.*

Because most people seem to be fairly limited in their exercise program after twenty, Yoga is highly recommended. It can be adopted by the young and old alike, as well as being something which can be practiced almost anywhere.

Actually the word ''Yoga'' means ''yoke between God and Man.'' One advantage is that it begins in improving the body, and extends into meditation and spiritual awareness. Furthermore, no one who ever practices Yoga in a class can be neurotic, for it is truly a yoke with God and not with the self!

---

* See Colleen Street's latest book, YOGA ANYONE? A STEP-by-STEP PICTURE BOOK FOR ALL. Available from the Miami Center.

Noel emphasizing a point at a lecture in New York.

Noel and his wife Colleen pose for each other during a
quick break between healing and past-life reading appoint-
ments in their hotel room in Phoenix, Arizona.

After Mrs. Street opened her own Yoga school in Miami, it was a real joy to see her students improving in the postures and generally experiencing a glow of good health.

Swami Vishnu Devananda, who runs two ashrams in Canada and the Bahamas, also notices that his students invariably respond quite favorably after a two-week session of Yoga, right breathing, and right diet.

5. *Church Attendance*

Someone once remarked, "It's good to go to church because there you find the other fellow has a sack of rocks just as big as yours!" Furthermore, a time set aside for worship in a temple is a break from the "I am" in our nature into the "Thou art!" of our spiritual consciousness, as we worship in spirit and truth.

Some people love to attend church, while others *need* the discipline of regular worship. Many people exclaim, "I don't get anything from church," and they go away feeling rather justified. But there is a spiritual law which prevents anyone from receiving spiritually, before he has given; the giving comes first! And the supporting of a church by one's presence is the first step.

There once was a lovely little Mexican church down on the Brazos River in Texas called St. Francis. Having always had a special love for these brown-skinned people, I was delighted when a friend invited me to go with him to that particular church.

Arriving for the Early Mass, we entered the door

and proceeded with the order of worship, they in Spanish, and I in English.

Many of these people had come to the church, poverty stricken and poor in body, but their humility and love clothed them in light as they worshipped their Lord. The sound of their voices ringing out in gratitude and thanksgiving, sapped my heart with its Spirit of universal truth. And I left the Mass that day, rich with a new awareness of the Cosmic Christ.

Indeed, one receives back from Spirit much more than he could ever give!

6. *Possess Nothing*

To "possess nothing" may quite well be a revolutionary thought to some people. Yet until we are willing to give up everything in our lives, we cannot become spiritually enhanced. Most of us forget, however, that as we release, so we are duly rewarded with a much greater spiritual satisfaction and power.

One of the obvious obstructions in our way is the accumulation of material things. There is a story in the New Testament, Matthew 19:16-22, wherein a young man approaches Christ and asks what thing he can do to have eternal life. And Jesus instructed that he must keep the commandments. "But the young man saith unto him, all these things have I kept from my youth up; what lack I yet? Jesus said unto him, if thou wilt be perfect, go and sell all that thou hast and give it to the poor . . . . But when the young man heard that saying, he went away sorrowful; for he had great possessions."

The Maori people have a lovely custom. When

someone comes into their homes and admires some object, they readily give it to the admirer, truly wanting him to have it. Likewise, they themselves receive even more in the spirit of giving. When we are so unencumbered by possessions, then we are free in the realm of the material world.

Sometimes the more subtle magnetic ties are harder to combat in the long run. These issues which were discussed earlier may entail sex, alcohol, drugs, power, personal relationships with other people, ad infinitum. . . .

A friend named Marge was required in her lifetime to give up all the things that had spelled security for her in a material and emotional sense, to the point of losing her entire family for awhile. Yet this test in her life was the very source of her spiritual awakening. Finally, her children did return to her and were amazed at the change in her nature.

Perhaps her greatest gift to me was her tranquility and calm which seemed to surround her in spite of the circumstances, and I asked her where she had gained her strength. With great contentment in her voice, she explained, "The greatest thing I have learned in this life is to possess nothing. It is much like grasping a handful of sand — as we clench our fist in an effort to hold it, it inevitably sifts out and is lost. But when we learn to scoop it into our palms and hold it upright, outstretched to all, then it is ours as long as we want it." This simple principle continues to change Marge's life in every area, as she truly possesses nothing, yet is spiritually rich.

Even any desire to achieve in the spiritual life is a shadow of ambition which must be lost, before

we ". . . come into fullness of the stature of Christ."
To seek to develop one's psychic gifts quickly, for
example, may be a form of self-aggrandizement which
needs checking, for "possession" is very cunning and
quite able to evade us at our blind spots.

Everyone must reach a point in his development
where he stands alone before God, without support of
any kind except a complete reliance and faith in
Spirit. And many tests will come to the aspirant on
the Pathway, until his progress has been proven.

So to hold *anything* is to separate us from our
full spiritual potential. The only real security in our
lives is spiritual substance, and as we begin to awaken
and believe this truth, we will ultimately release all
things which bind us. And possessing nothing, we
shall be fully free.

7. *Thank God for Problems*

With the multiplicity of problems which beset the
human race, one could argue, "I wouldn't be under
so much pressure if it weren't for this thing or that
thing in my life." But living a problem-free life is the
Utopia for which we earthlings were not made. We
come into incarnation to learn lessons which the physical life can teach us, and as we face and overcome
our karma, we, likewise, grow spiritually. So, in
truth, our problems are really opportunities to use
the capacity of our spirit.

What about the person whose karma is difficult?
There are many people who are confronted with a
situation which they may not even be able to change,
but in truly thanking God for the problem, the power
is removed and a reversal in attitude occurs.

If our karma happens to be some physical ailment which has not responded to treatment, how can we react? I know a young woman who has spent the last twenty-five years confined to a wheelchair due to a case of poliomyelitis when she was a child. The paralysis left her completely dependent on others in a physical sense, so that throughout her school years she had to attend a special class for the handicapped. Her courage and her cheerfulness has constantly been her strength, and last year she completed her Master's degree at a large university. Today she teaches the eighth grade from her wheelchair, and she exudes the warmth and love of a devoted teacher. How rich her spirit has grown in this experience. From Psalm 126:5 comes the verse, "They that sow in tears shall reap in joy."

So even though we may not be able to alter the circumstances of our lives, we *do* have the option of changing our attitudes toward them. Eventually, a new harmony will spring forth from our beings, achieving good for ourselves and others.

8. *Enjoy Life in Total*

Most of us would probably be jarred if we stopped and counted the moments we lose each day through lack of awareness. Quite easily the cares of the physical life can snatch away our attention, and with it go the opportunities to feed our spirits. Upon examining the situation, we inevitably find that the thief has come through the door of our own negligence.

True enjoyment of life is composed of the simplest things — the laughter of children, the song of a bird, the glory of sunset against the winter sky. And in realizing these moments, we soon find that our hearts pound with a new vitality and joy. At last, we know that we are one with the whole Universe, and all striving can cease.

It is this inner quality of contentment that is so evident in the life of Noel Street, the Psychic Healer. From his appreciation of "little" things has grown a full awareness of Spirit, leading him daily into higher pathways. Through him the Light of Healing has flowed freely into the world. It can flow through you, too, in ever-increasing degrees of fullness through service and love.

Glossary of Sub-titles

235